Net Words

Net Words
Creating High-Impact Online Copy

Nick Usborne

McGraw-Hill

New York Chicago San Francisco Lisbon London
Madrid Mexico City Milan New Delhi
San Juan Seoul Singapore Sydney Toronto

McGraw-Hill

A Division of The McGraw·Hill Companies

1 2 3 4 5 6 7 8 9 0 DOC/DOC 0 9 8 7 6 5 4 3 2 1

ISBN 0-07-138039-6

Printed and bound by R. R. Donnelly & Sons Company.
Designed by Michael Mendelsohn at MM Design 2000, Inc.

McGraw-Hill books are available at special quantity discounts to use as premiums and sales promotions, or for use in corporate training programs. For more information, please write to the Director of Special Sales, Professional Publishing, McGraw-Hill, Two Penn Plaza, New York, NY 10121-2298. Or contact your local bookstore.

To my four sons,
Matthew, Daniel, Benjamin, and Thomas.

And in memory of
my father and of my brother, Robert.

Contents

Contents

Foreword

A few days after I finished reading the manuscript for *Net Words*, I happened to visit the Web site of one of the major airlines. "our mission is to ensure that our customers accomplish theirs," the company's CEO greeted me. "We are committed to continually improving our brand product and focusing on customer service. Every employee has been trained to deliver our unique brand of customer service. Our Customer Service Plan is specifically designed to assist us in reaching this objective for every customer on every flight."

Boy, could they use Nick Usborne's book.

Why can't they talk like real people? (and what's a "brand of customer service" anyway)? As Nick would point out, this type of generic corporate speak is not going to work—especially not online, where your voice is the main thing that sets you apart from the crowd.

Of course, words don't live in a vacuum. I've had a couple of bad experiences with that particular airline, so when I read what the CEO had to say about its commitment to customer service, what went through my mind was, "Yeah, right." A reader's reaction to your words depends on everything from how she was greeted by your receptionist to what she heard about you from her friends.

Can good writing cover up for bad service or a lousy product? Usborne says it best: "Great copywriting cannot be used as a bandage to obscure the way that you really are."

When your customers compare notes via email, chat rooms, and newsgroups, you can't hide what's really going on.

But great copy *can* make a difference. The words that you use online are, in fact, a critical part of the user's experience, and Nick packs the book with examples of how to write online text that is funny, personal, engaging, and informative—in short, how to write text that people actually want to read.

I hope that someone from that airline will read *Net Words*. I hope that *everyone* who writes online will read this book. We could all learn from it. As I read the manuscript, I found myself rewriting emails I was about to send out and changing some text on my Web site. Usborne will make you think, and he'll remind you of some basics that so many of us tend to forget when we write: Be personal, keep it simple, be specific.

What I love about this book is that it is a practical guide, not a manifesto. Usborne provides his own useful advice, as well as words of wisdom from other people in the trenches. The book lists new rules along with some old ones. What do they have in common? They work and they make sense. Nick's objective is not to shock us but to help us do a better job. In the process, he has written a terrific book that should influence the way companies communicate with their customers online.

Emanuel Rosen
Menlo Park
August 2001

Acknowledgments

I 'm told that writing a book is a four-walled hell. For me, this hasn't been the case at all. Writing *Net Words* was almost entirely painless. I'd like to take credit for this myself, but the fear of being found out prevents me.

First, I would like to thank my wife, Julie, who read the manuscript numerous times and identified all the places where I'd missed things, repeated myself, and generally messed up. Thank you.

Second, I'd like to thank my editor at McGraw-Hill, Michelle Williams. Michelle, somehow, has left me with the impression that getting published is a breeze. I suspect this is because she's been doing all the hard work in the background, while I've been happily tapping away at the keyboard with my two typing fingers. Thank you.

Introduction

Nobody is paying close enough attention to the words on ecommerce sites. This is a shame, as great copy can address some of the most pressing challenges facing your business online.

What can you do to make your business online work harder? How can you make more sales, keep more customers, and better insulate yourself from the competition? And how can you move forward and make immediate improvements to your online business without running the risk of making some horrendous, high-tech, doomed-to-failure investment?

One answer to these and other key questions has been staring us in the face since the first commercial sites sprang up on the Web. Work harder on the words—the words on your site, in your emails, in your newsletters, and in your customer service correspondence.

Ask offline marketers about the power of words. They'll tell you how changing just a single phrase or word in a sales letter can significantly impact the response rate achieved. Ask the writers of TV commercials and print ads for newspapers and magazines. The world of offline commerce understands only too well the impact of words. But this isn't the case online. The attention of marketers online is focused on the technologies that deliver the messages, not on the messages themselves.

One of the ironies here is that the environment itself—the Internet—is all about text. It always has been. It started as brief conversations between the technically savvy. The Net—and then the Web—has always been about connecting with other individuals, connecting and sharing. Even today, in the hopeful world of broadband and wireless, people talk with one another through their keyboards far more frequently than they go to a commerce-enabled Web site. Over 350 million people around the world are online to share words, and only occasionally to go shopping. Everyone except for those who are doing business online knows that the Web is about words. Words are its lifeblood and its pulse.

The trouble is, this simple truth is intolerable to every software designer, "solution" provider, financial analyst, venture capitalist, and elitist pundit on the planet. Where's the glamour in words? How can you invest in them? How can you own them? Where's the upswing? Where's the glory? And how can something as revolutionary as the Internet be dominated by something as mundane, as old, and as ordinary as words?

What's important to business online right now is to start showing some strong results. And while great copy online can't cure all your ills, it can certainly make a big difference.

- Good writing can differentiate your business from its many competitors online.

- Good writing can increase sales from your site, improving conversion rates where they matter most.

- Good writing can increase customer loyalty by making sure that your personalization efforts really are personal.

- Good writing can bring your customer service to life, connecting with customers much more effectively.

- Good writing can make your name and message stand out in an area that is becoming increasingly busy—your customers' email inboxes.

Each chapter in this book will give you some immediate recommendations that you can apply to your business online, for a very nominal investment of time and money. That's the good news.

The bad news is that there are a number of barriers to getting great copy written for your online business. It's no accident that you don't have a copywriter among your senior online managers. It's no accident that when the site development group sits around the table, nobody says, "Hang on, we can't get started without the writer."

Until now, writers have not been included as key players in the Web site or business development process. As a result, other participants in the process have come to believe that words don't play a very important role. So there's some history to get past, some convictions and assumptions at which to chip away. As a result of their exclusion from the development of the early online businesses, there is a significant lack of great copywriters with deep online expertise and experience. And those copywriters that have been hurriedly drafted in from their duties as advertisement and brochure writers often don't understand the unique demands of writing for commerce online. (The term "copywriter" is used quite deliberately. Copywriters are the people who use words to encourage customer actions and make commerce work. And that's what this book is about. Using words to do business online.)

Who should read this book? Two groups. The first and primary group includes all those doing business online who are looking to increase sales, improve customer loyalty, or find ways to differentiate themselves from their dozens of competitors. The second group includes the people from development groups, advertising agencies, and marketing consultancy groups who need a better understanding of how copy works online and how to make it work harder. And, of course, for everyone who is hoping to write great copy on the Web.

Finally, examples have been taken from a number of sites and email campaigns to illustrate a variety of points being made in this book. At the time of writing, the example text was as it appears in this book. Since that time, a number of the examples used will have been updated or changed.

Finally, when this book suggests that a particular site or email is flawed in some way, no disrespect is meant to its creators. Goodness knows, it's been tough enough getting it right online in the early years. Mistakes are a good thing. They are the trail of crumbs that help those who follow get it right (and then make their own mistakes further along the way). The various examples on these pages have been chosen not to praise some and denigrate others, but simply to illustrate the points this book is trying to communicate.

CHAPTER ONE

EVERYTHING CHANGES ONLINE

Why Copywriting Online Is Different

Without great copy, commerce would be dead on its feet. Nothing is ever bartered, traded, or sold without words. Whether in print, on the TV, or by word of mouth, words make the sale. This is as true on the Web as it is in the offline world.

However, the language of making that sale online needs to be different. The Web and its history demand that companies recognize and use a different approach, a different voice, and a different attitude when they sell online. You can't write online in the same way that you write a sales letter, brochure, or radio script. It simply doesn't work. Being slow to recognize these differences has proved to be the undoing of many an online venture.

To create a unique and powerful presence, you first need to understand why the voice of business online is so often off-key right now. And why, online, it is so important to get that voice right. It is the online environment's sensitivity to voice and tone that dictates the enormous care you must take with the way in which you write.

When companies speak and write to consumers online in the same way as they communicate through offline advertising media, they are making a fundamental mistake. First, the Internet is not a marketing channel or an advertising medium in any traditional sense. Second, the audience you are writing to is no longer just an audience. It is composed of active participants and co-owners of the same environment through which you are trying to market your goods and services.

With differences as fundamental as these, it comes as no surprise that when you attempt to do business in this environment, you have to make some big adjustments.

How Everything Started to Change.

To understand the need to write to online audiences differently, take a look at the Net's history. The story began in the late seventies and eighties with the arrival of Bulletin Board Systems, Usenet, and more narrowly focused services like The Well. With these new services, it was possible to communicate knowledge, news, and unedited opinions with hundreds and then thousands of other people who shared common interests. Back then, if you knew someone with a bit of tech savvy, a computer, and a couple of modems, you could get online and start sharing. These systems were free and slowly started growing.

In his 1993 book, *Virtual Community*, Howard Rheingold describes Usenet as:

> . . . a place for conversation or publication, like a giant coffeehouse with a thousand rooms; it is also a worldwide digital version of the Speakers Corner in London's Hyde Park, an unedited collection of letters to the editor, a floating flea market, a huge

vanity publisher, and a collection of every odd special-interest group in the world.

Usenet gave people a voice that they had never had before. This new, open communication arena was not owned by the media. It was and is wonderfully decentralized and shared by millions. By the end of the year 2000 there were about 27,000 active newsgroups on Usenet, with approximately 675,000 messages being posted each day.

Running parallel to the growth of Usenet were some early attempts to make a business based on gathering communities together online. One of the first contenders, CompuServe, was launched at the beginning of the eighties and, by the decade's end, boasted a membership of over 500,000. Describing themselves as "The information Service you won't outgrow," they took aim at a fairly sophisticated market. In contrast, Prodigy, launched under that name in 1988, was aimed at a far broader, more popular audience. As was AOL, launched under that now familiar name in 1989.

As the eighties came to a close, what was once a fairly closed environment, available only to a few, was opening its doors to a much wider audience. The variety of voices to be heard across online communities was growing by leaps and bounds. The Internet had slowly passed into the public, popular domain.

For today's marketers it's important to recognize not only that individuals arrived online before companies did, but that it was those individuals who formed and created the language and etiquette of online communication. There was no Strunk and White guide to online style and grammar. The tone and delivery wasn't determined behind closed doors on Madison Avenue. What happened was the growth of a style that evolved, and is still evolving, beneath the fingertips of millions of individuals online. It was keyboard rap. Emails and posts were usually brief and to the point. Patience with newcomers was slight.

Does this mean that marketers have to use the same style and language? Should companies masquerade as hip individuals online? Of course not. But as any company that serves foreign markets knows, you ignore local cultures at your peril. And yes, to traditional corporations, the Internet is a foreign country.

Consumers Become Connected through Online Communities.

The creation of virtual communities online was fed by a basic human desire to be heard. For the first time, instead of just talking with one's family, priest, and friends, it was possible to listen to, speak to, and share with thousands of other people, regardless of distance. First "lurking" and then tentatively raising their voices, new arrivals at discussion groups or forums felt their way into the community. Indeed, the FAQ sections that newcomers are still encouraged to read before posting often advise the "newbie" to listen first and contribute later. It's important to listen, not only to avoid endless repetition of the same popular subjects and themes, but also to learn the particular tone and voice of that group. This is a sensitivity to tone that you don't come across in the offline world. Once part of the group and accepted by one's peers, it's time to participate and enjoy.

At what other time could regular people contribute to the collective wisdom of a large group on such a large scale over such wide distances? Posts and discussions are more than just transient conversations; they are content that has value, living on in vast archives.

One of the keys to inclusion in these communities was that process of lurking and listening before jumping in. If there was a price of entry, that price was to show enough respect to learn the language of the group before opening your mouth. Newcomers to the Internet learned this courtesy early on. If they didn't, there were always plenty of veterans of the Net who were willing and happy to shout them down and flame them into submission. There was a code, and you had to stick to it.

When companies began to view the Internet as some kind of new sales channel, many didn't make the effort to read the FAQs of this new space. They didn't pause long enough to find out a little about the unique culture of this strange new land. Or more accurately, they were too complacent to imagine that there was any medium through which they could not raise their voices, boast their promises, and not have everyone sit quietly and listen.

The Consumer Becomes a Participant for the First Time.

Before the Internet, the only voices heard outside of your immediate community of family, friends, and colleagues were the voices of the media—TV, newspapers, radio, billboards, magazines, direct mail. Big companies wanted to reach you with their messages—make "impressions"—and the media grew accordingly in order to deliver these impressions. Communication was a one-way street, a monologue. No customer ever had the opportunity to participate in the process.

Mass marketing worked well not only because the available media had tremendous reach, but also because each prospective customer was reached as an isolated, passive individual. That is to say, when you sat in front of your TV and an automobile manufacturer told you that its latest sedan was the best in its class, that was the only voice and opinion immediately available to you. If you were particularly interested, you might go to the newsstand and buy a magazine or two for a second and third opinion. Or ask a neighbor. But most of the time, across multiple media, consumers were exposed to persuasive, repetitive messages that effectively formed their impressions and opinions of the goods and services they paid for every day. The math behind mass marketing worked just fine. The more impressions you made on your audience, the more products you sold.

Consumers Become Better Connected and Informed.

First with the arrival of Usenet and now with dozens of price comparison and "reputation manager" sites available to surfers, some key characteristics of the advertiser's audience have changed.

With hundreds of millions of people online, visiting numerous sites and forums through which they can compare products and services, the corporate marketing voice is under greater scrutiny than ever before. Now, when you broadcast an advertising message to people who are connected online, you are no longer writing or talking to a single, isolated individual. Tell someone your sedan is the best in its class, and suddenly that person can access the opinions of thousands of other people.

>> Hey, guys, I've heard good things about this vehicle. What do you think?

>> I don't know. I read something about some recalls. You might want to check it out.

For the first time, the voice of the manufacturer is not the only sound to be heard. The consumer is no longer at the mercy of corporate brochures and silver-tongued salespeople. In fact, every connected consumer has become a participant in the creation and dissemination of advertising messages. And by inclination, most connected consumers will find the opinions of their online peers more trustworthy than the promises of the manufacturer.

The trouble is, although the landscape has changed absolutely, companies are still using copy on their sites that may have suited a mass-marketing medium, but is no longer appropriate for the Internet.

Here's an illustration of the disjoint between the voice of the company and the ears of the consumer. The following text is taken from a Honda Web site and describes Honda's Prelude sports car:

> The Honda Prelude is the true essence of a high-performance driving machine. From its low, wide stance to its wind-defying body, the Prelude delivers sizzling performance in an absolutely refined way. In fact, everything Honda engineers have learned on the racetrack they've lavished on the Prelude. Like its aluminum alloy VTEC engine and its sophisticated 4-wheel independent double-wishbone suspension.

Anyone with experience in the automotive marketing business will recognize this copy for what it is. It is brochure copy. If you read through a few brochures from your local car dealership, whatever the manufacturer, you will begin to discern a particular style and genre. Statements like "the Prelude delivers sizzling performance in an absolutely refined way" are typical of that genre and may or may not be good copy when it comes to selling the vehicle from the pages of a glossy brochure. But when you take that copy and paste it into your Web site, you're about as in sync as a McDonald's hamburger franchise in rural France. It just doesn't fit. There's no cultural connection. And as with McDonald's in France, when companies show an ignorance of and indifference to the culture in which they operate, the natives become irritated and restless.

For a guide to how the natives speak, all Honda needs to do is head to one of the numerous online discussion lists devoted to its cars and read posts like this one.

> . . . good choice getting the prelude. I was so tempted to get the Interga, but I couldn't be more happy about the prelude. So are there any mods on the car yet? what's the first thing your going to do?

Or:

> Well, I was looking for a leather shift knob for my base lude and I wanted the one that comes in the SH, but the dealership wanted about $125 for it, after some very brief thinking about it I decided to try and order one from the states. Couldn't have been a better idea. It cost me $80 for the shift knob and a new front emblem, plus $20 delivery. So I saved about $45 (when you consider the taxes applied when buying here). And guess what!?! I got a red stitched one! It looks awesome.

The language may be casual, but the writers clearly love their cars and are unlikely to be impressed by superficial copy like "the Prelude delivers sizzling performance in an absolutely refined way." Different style, different culture. You can't just cut and paste the text you used in last year's brochure. For the Web, you need to rewrite and get the correct tone for each new context.

A Cautionary Tale of Two Lawyers from Arizona.

Marketers are sometimes puzzled by how people respond to marketing over the Internet. After all, most of us receive yards and yards of junk mail and catalogs every year, with barely a whimper. Junk in, junk out.

People may not much like unsolicited mail, but they tend not to get too upset about it either. That's why direct marketers keep sending those amazing, special offers. And they're not foolish—they know the math is in their favor. Sure, ninety-eight out of a hundred won't respond to their mailing, but when the last two people do, they spend enough money to make it all worthwhile.

It was only a matter of time, as more and more people came online during the early nineties, before someone had the idea of bulk mailing over the Internet. The most celebrated and first example of unsolicited bulk emailing, or spam, took place in 1994. Two Arizona lawyers, Laurence Canter and Martha Siegel, posted an advertisement to Usenet. The "Green Card Spam," as it came to be known, changed Usenet forever. From that day on, every discussion list, forum, and personal inbox has been fighting to keep unsolicited commercial messages at bay.

Canter and Siegel went on to write *How to Make a Fortune on the Information Superhighway*, sharing their knowledge with thousands of other would-be spammers. But their activities did not go unnoticed. There was an immediate and angry outcry against them and anyone else who did the same. Unfortunately, the outcry didn't change much, and the flood of spam online has continued to increase.

But online marketers should take note of the reaction of the online communities. This was not business as usual. This was not like direct mail. People clearly had different feelings—and continue to have those feelings—when exposed to pushy, unsolicited messages online.

No, the Internet Is Not an Advertising Medium.

If you have seen the children's movie *102 Dalmations*, you will probably remember the talking macaw, Waddlesworth. Waddlesworth is convinced that he is a rottweiler dog. He barks and talks, but doesn't fly. After all, rottweilers don't fly. Toward the end of the movie, one of the dalmation puppies is in mortal danger and, in spite of himself, Waddlesworth takes to the air, flies to the rescue, picks up the hapless puppy by the collar, and crash-lands a hero. He picks himself up and speaks. (The voice belongs to Eric Idle of Monty Python fame.) "I just realized," he says, "I'm not a rottweiler at all. . . ." At this point everyone in the audience smiles in anticipation of this moment of self-discovery. But instead, Waddlesworth continues, "I'm a retriever!"

Without question, it's the best line in the movie. In the online environment, one might imagine the Madison Avenue advertising executive experiencing a similar epiphany. "Hang on," he says. "The Internet isn't a brand-building medium at all!" At this point you might wish he would say something like, "The Internet isn't any kind of advertising medium. It's a vast network of connected communities and individuals!" But no, our exec continues, "It's a direct-marketing medium!"

As with Waddlesworth, a lot of marketers miss the point completely. Unfortunately, in the case of many marketers, there's no comic relief to help us make light of their lack of awareness.

To call the Internet an advertising medium makes about as much sense as saying the same about New York City. Yes, you can advertise in many different ways within the city, but New York is a great deal more than just an advertising medium. It's a huge population, broken into distinct communities with an infinitely complex set of interconnections among individuals, corporations, and government.

The same is true of the Internet. It's much more like a massive, global city and not at all like any kind of traditional advertising medium. Sure, you can promote and sell your products there, but to do it well you first need to understand what makes this particular city tick.

A Shared Environment Needn't Force Marketers to Be Passive.

On the one hand there are those traditional marketers who see the Internet simply as another advertising medium and pound away with the same old, one-way messages. Their approach is flawed, and the language they use in their promotions demonstrates their lack of understanding and lack of respect for an online, interactive audience.

On the other hand, many self-proclaimed online experts have swung to the opposite extreme. They say that instead of marketers taking the initiative and advertising their products and services to prospective customers, they should take a more passive role and wait for their prospects to approach them with requests for information. In other words, companies should make themselves available online, but not push themselves out into the shared space of the Net. There is some sense and logic to these ideas. Huge aggregators of customer opinions and knowledge such as Usenet, Planet-Feedback, and Bizrate become the middlemen through which customers control their choices and decide on which companies to approach to satisfy their needs of the day.

This approach sits very well within the interactive, shared, and common space of the Web. It gives control to the customer, and it enables and encourages the free flow of information and opinions among millions of customers. But is it really reasonable or desirable for companies to sit on their thumbs and do nothing, leaving their future and the jobs of their employees in the hands of some third-party aggregators online? Not for a nanosecond.

There is no question that companies online have to adjust their offline habits. They do have to recognize that this is a quite different business environment. It is a shared space. Their customers and prospects do have a great deal more control and power online. But with that said, companies can and should work just as hard to ensure their success online. There is no need to be passive, and it's not even certain that customers want companies to be silent online. If what you have to offer is of real value and if you approach and address your audience with respect for their time and attention, they'll likely welcome your messages.

Can the Voices of Corporations Be Sincere?

This question was inspired by a conversation with David Weinberger, one of the authors of *The Cluetrain Manifesto*. In answer to the suggestion that companies can talk to their customers in a voice that is genuine and sincere, David posed the following:

> Suppose the marketing VP asks Beth, a marketing staffer, to write copy for the site. She comes up with a fantastic piece of copywriting: heartfelt, funny, human, truthful, frank. Everyone loves it. Sure enough, the day it's posted, there's an increase in clickthroughs and sales. This continues for a couple of weeks. Then the marketing VP suggests that they try testing various tweaks. So, for two days 50% of the visitors see a version that changes Beth's word "spiffy" to "bitchin'." Sure enough, the clickthroughs and sales go up. Next they test changing "ultimate" to "extreme" because maybe that will skew younger. The stats show no change, but when they change it to "xtreme" there's a significant increase. The testing and tweaking continues.
>
> At what point is this no longer the expression of a human voice? And isn't this inevitable? And does it matter? Does the fact that the copy came from a real individual with a real passion for the product ever matter? Suppose Beth changes her mind about the product. Does the original posting now have to come down? Suppose she changes jobs. If it doesn't matter if the original posting no longer represents a real human being's thoughts and way of talking, then does it matter that at one point it did? Can corporations be sincere? Can they be authentic?

The scenario described above is completely credible. Beth's approach and voice may do a fabulous job of connecting with the company's customers and may build a loyal following. Yes, her company will want to test the copy. Copy should always be tested. But if a variation on the control text results in an immediate increase in subscriptions or sales, that doesn't mean that the change should automatically be applied. It's easy to increase response rates. Just add the words, "One in five chance to win a Palm PDA. Click here!" The response rate jumps. But the quality of attention you receive will be diminished. So the question a marketer should ask when looking at the test results on Beth's copy is, "Hang on, the results are better with the new copy, but what are we losing? Are we losing credibility? Are we reducing our chances of keeping this customer in the long term? Should I go for the short-term fix or the longer-term play?" Not an easy decision. Particularly not at a time, as Dr. Weinberger points out, when pursuit of "shareholder value" is the prevailing Holy Grail.

Another point about Beth's copy. It shouldn't be in Beth's voice. It's not credible for a company to speak with the voice of an individual. Beth's skill will be to find and articulate a voice that is consistent with the company's real nature and also rings true for the customer. Finding the intersection point of those two elements is where the writer's focus should be. So if Beth switches jobs or changes her mind about the product and someone else takes over the writing, the new person can still continue to work and write in the company's voice.

And now for the answer to David Weinberger's final questions, "Can corporations be sincere? Can they be authentic?" In all honesty, there will be times when they cannot. Within any but the smallest of companies, a company's responsibility is, like it or not, to its shareholders, whether those shares be held privately or publicly. One would hope that companies would consider that being honest and sincere with their customers should always be in alignment with their corporate goals. But that's not always the case, and as consumers, the members of the public know it.

Which brings us to the subject of the relationship between the creators and the recipients of marketing messages. When you're told that a particular detergent will make your clothes whiter than white, you know that it's not true. You can't get whiter than white. When you're told that you will have an "organic" experience, moaning and all, with a particular shampoo, you know that's not true either. Nor will buying a particular beer put you in the company of beautiful young men and women. So are consumers being deceived? Or are they smarter than that? Of course they're smarter than that. Marketers and consumers dance together within a world of fiction created by the marketer and played out by the consumer. It's part of the consumer culture.

But that dance has unspoken rules. Consumers will recognize and play along with the notion that shampoo can give you an "organic" experience. It's part of the game. But they won't tolerate outright deceit or sneakiness. Offline, this game has been played for decades; the rules are understood and continue to shift and evolve. Online, it's still early in regard to determining the nature of the dance, but one thing is for sure—the rules that apply offline do not apply online. It's a new dance with new rules, and companies have to be sensitive to all the different elements that contribute to and influence their gradual evolution.

Learning How to Write Online.

There are some key elements to treating your online audience with respect. One of these is the well-known and clearly defined practice of permission marketing, as outlined by Seth Godin in his book of the same name. But another key element, not covered in that book or any other, is the use of great writing. You can't write to your audience in the same style and manner as you do offline. Nor should you be entirely passive with your text. You're online to do business, and that should be reflected in the copy that is found on every page of your site and within every email you send out.

Recognize that to succeed online you need to work with a whole new set of disciplines and skills in the arena of copywriting. It's OK to be aggressive with your plans. It's OK to want to drive more traffic, improve conversion rates, build loyalty, and make your company stand out from all the others.

Great copy can help you achieve all these ends on the Web. In fact, one can argue that great copy is the best and most economical and enduring way to achieve these ends. But to create great copy, an investment has to be made in learning a new way to write for the online environment.

CHAPTER TWO

ALLOW COPYWRITERS TO DO GREAT WORK

Copywriting Online Is Not Bad

To achieve great writing online, copywriters first need to have the authority and freedom to do good work. If a copywriter is accorded little respect within a Web development group, there is almost no chance that he or she will be able to make significant improvements to a homepage, shopping cart, newsletter, email program, or any other element of your online efforts.

This is one of the major impediments to the writing of great copy online right now—too little respect is given to copywriters and their work. To copywriters from the offline world, this is a puzzling state of affairs. Advertising agency copywriters are used to being shown tremendous respect. They are held in esteem not just for their writing expertise, but also for their marketing knowledge and insights. The best of them become creative directors and wield huge influence over the entire creative product of the agency. Good copywriters have a way of solving commercial challenges with unique, creative solutions. So it's not surprising that when those copywriters start working online, they are puzzled to find themselves excluded from the inner sanctum of decision makers.

Looking at the problem of language and the Web, Julia Hayden, a user interface engineer, notes:

> Language is the tool we use to filter and define the world. It's our first and most powerful tool, and separates us from the armadillos of the world. Language enables us to make connections, to build complexities, and to influence each other.
>
> It also has the power to divide us: it crystalizes our differences, and helps us antagonize and irritate each other.
>
> Why do we—as web-builders—overlook even the most basic aspects of language so frequently when we build our sites? Is language so transparent in our lives that we fail to recognize its importance? Do we even think about it at all? If we do, who manages the language in our sites?

How has the industry arrived at this state of affairs? How has the Web grown up with such a broad disrespect for the copywriter's skills and contribution? What has driven us to exclude the very people who are best qualified to answer some of the greatest challenges ecommerce faces today? The answers to those questions are complicated, to say the least. But they need to be addressed if the industry is to move forward.

The origins of the Web do not lie in commerce. The genesis of the Internet—and then the Web—was overseen by academics and the technically gifted. The infrastructure and the culture of the Web were, for many years, deliberately anticommerce. Deep within the fabric of the Web, you can still find a pervading view that marketing online is uncouth. Many online "experts" hold unspoken thoughts about copywriters being manipulative, inherently dishonest, and untrustworthy. In the late nineties, even after the whole idea of ecommerce was accepted, it still held true that to "sound like you're selling" was frowned upon by the Internet's early adopters. In their unwritten code, it was OK to build the mechanism by which the Web delivered its messages, but not OK to write the messages themselves.

The persistence of the attitude that marketing writers are hacks and irrelevant to the online experience is more damaging that one might imagine. Just because the Web is an interactive environment across which all voices can be heard doesn't mean that a business site can't benefit dramatically from the skills of a good copywriter. The best copywriters listen carefully and then articulate a simple message that genuinely touches on interests shared by both the company and its customers. It can be done.

Cynicism about marketing online may be good for a quick laugh over a beer or two, but its longer-term effect is corrosive. And that's bad for everyone looking to do business online. This passage from *The Cluetrain Manifesto*, written by Christopher Locke, Rick Levine, Doc Searls, and David Weinberger, expresses a common and popular frustration with "marketing-speak":

> [T]here is no demand for messages. The customer doesn't want to hear from your business, thank you very much. The message that gets broadcast to you, me, and the rest of the earth's population has nothing to do with me in particular. It's worse than noise. It's an interruption. It's the Anti-Conversation.

For much of the time, customers are right to feel fed up and frustrated by the written messages they receive from companies. Yes, those messages are often irrelevant, unclear, and unwelcome. But that doesn't mean copywriting is the spawn of Satan. It just means that *bad* copywriting is the spawn of Satan.

By way of comparison to the *Cluetrain* viewpoint, here is a quite different one, expressed by one of America's most respected copywriters, Ed McCabe:

> To me, all advertising that is truly great reeks of honest humanity. Between every word you can smell the hot breath of the writer. Whether a result of wit, intelligence, insight or artfulness, great advertising invariably transmits itself to the receiver on a fragile human frequency.
>
> Source: *The Copywriter's Bible*, AD & AD Mastercraft Series.

It's a shame that current online thinking finds it hard to imagine that a copywriter could possibly have the sensitivity to write on a "fragile human frequency." Here's another interesting observation that brings the craft of copywriter in very close alignment with the *Cluetrain* vision of what marketing should be:

> That way I can write copy the way I believe all copy should be written: as a conversation between two human beings rather than an announcement from manufacturer to consumer.
>
> Chris O'Shea, Copywriter
>
> Source: *The Copywriter's Bible*, AD & AD Mastercraft Series.

The craft of copywriting is not the enemy of those who aspire to a nonsense-free marketing environment online. Quite the reverse. It's the lack of professional writers and top-shelf talent with long experience online that has led to the voices of companies online coming over as insincere and inconsistent. The industry doesn't need less copywriting. It just needs better copywriting.

What, Then, Is the Role of the Copywriter Online?

While the role of the copywriter in the world of bricks and mortar is very clearly defined, the opposite is true on the

Web. What do copywriters do online—even when the question is confined within the area of marketing writing? Are they the people who write the product or service descriptions on your site? Are they the people who write the text that drives visitors forward from screen to screen? Are they also the people who write the outbound emails and newsletters? The customer service emails? And is copywriting always quite separate from the job of writing content on a site? If there are different types of writers with different skills, by how much and when should they overlap? Should there be specialists who focus simply on one narrow task, like increasing conversion rates from one screen to the next? Should there be writers who become masters of writing the text on shopping cart screens, where conversion rates tend to be poor?

These are questions that have barely been asked—let alone answered by many companies online. As a result, key parts of a site and the emails they generate are often written by a variety of different people. And as a result of that, the tone, quality, and direction of copy across the various media, platforms, and channels online are inconsistent. Inevitably, businesses online end up sounding like they suffer from a severe case of a multiple personality disorder. And none of those personalities appear to be particularly articulate or interesting. It's hard for a single, strong voice to ring through if you don't have a very senior writer at the helm, someone who is responsible for orchestrating all the different elements and writers within the organization.

Ideally, however many writers an online business employs, and whatever their specialties, they would all be professionals and all be under the direction of a chief copywriter or copy manager. The chief copywriter would have two main parts to his or her job: (1) to ensure the quality, efficacy, and consistency of all text across all channels and (2) to fight like hell in support of the writer's role within the online enterprise.

Copywriters: The Only People Online Not Free to Write.

It's ironic. The Web was and is the most text-centric of all business environments. The Net started with text through services like Usenet. Today it is still largely text-based, with hundreds of millions of people connecting with one another through email, discussion groups, and chat.

According to eMarketer, a major aggregator of Internet research, 97 million active email users sent 536 billion emails in 2000. By 2003, 140 million users will send 1.035 trillion emails. People online also like to chat with one another. Over 77 million people get together and share their thoughts and dreams through ICQ, with an additional 64 million using AOL's other messaging service, Instant Messenger. Not to mention the millions of personal homepages that people put up and share with family and friends. Or the millions of breathless communications that fly back and forth between connected game players. The online environment has liberated millions of people who never before had a voice. For the first time, Joe and Joanne Public can get online, get busy with their keyboards, and be heard.

Meanwhile, and here comes the irony, copywriters are often completely hamstrung and almost silent. How come? How is it that within the most text-based business environment ever conceived marketing writers have found no niche, no power, no voice? In large part, the answer to that lies in the fact that writers were not there when the party started. Writers didn't play a part in determining how the Web would work, how it would be structured, how information would be delivered. As a result, the power of words has not become one of the fundamental pillars used to build and hold up major commercial Web sites. Design is there, usability is there, information architecture is there, but copywriting is not.

When good writers are apparently so absent from the process, it's not surprising that online copywriters face challenges like this one, described by copywriter Peter Kaufman:

> I worked in a company that was 100% technical and operations focused until they realized that our clients buy creative and don't give a flip about how the SQL servers work. In the middle of a huge push to get a site done with no help available, one of the big honchos said, "Can't Jim help you?" "Jim," I reminded him was in Application Development. "But I've seen him write reports, he's good."

Or, in the words of site designer, Mary Ihla:

> It's probably happened to every professional Web designer—the client plops down their annual report, a handful of brochures, and maybe a catalog or two and says, "Here's our copy."

> They don't understand how writing for the Web differs from all other media, even direct mail. And, very few even consider copywriting as part of the Web development process.

While no malice or disrespect may be intended, development and marketing groups clearly aren't viewing copywriters, or, indeed, the copy on their sites, as being central to their success. The delivery and the presentation of the message are accorded a great deal of investment and attention, but not the message itself.

Usability Engineers Should Be the Copywriter's Best Friend.

When much of the culture and structure of the commercial Web was built, usability engineers were on the guest list, but copywriters were not. Usability engineers had had many years learning their craft in the field of software development, and so it was only a small move to step over and become experts on the Web. These are the people who want to make it easier for visitors to find their way around your site. Usability engineers have one of the toughest jobs of all. Their job is critical because users hate complicated sites that are cluttered, confusing, and spiced up with unnecessary animations and the like. Within the environment of the Web, with small screen sizes and slow download speeds, it isn't easy to keep things simple. Designers and programmers may find it hard to resist the latest plug-ins. Marketers and CEOs may apply pressure to make the site "cutting edge." Vendors will try to sell you 3D animation software, voice-over live chat applications, and other bandwidth and attention-hungry elements.

Underlying the temptation to make sites overly complicated is the fact that certainly in the late nineties, investors liked to see their sites being state-of-the-art. Web site founders knew this and recognized that it was harder to raise capital for a site that looked too simple and had no bells and whistles. Shareholder value stood in the way of usability. In short, the job of the usability expert is both very important and tough. He or she is fighting constantly to make sites easier to use for the only group of people that really matters, the site visitors.

The most influential of the online usability engineers, Jakob Nielsen, also recognizes the importance of copy on the Web. The following is a short excerpt taken from his book, *Designing Web Usability*:

> When writing for the web, you're not only affecting the content, you're affecting the core user experience because users look at the text and the headlines first. Although it's important to be grammatically correct, it's also important to present the content in a manner that draws in readers.

That's absolutely correct. So it's unfortunate, as Mary Ihla points out, that among key members of the development groups, which often include a usability engineer, "very few even consider copywriting as part of the Web development process." How can great copy become a key element of the user experience if the copywriter is not even included in the process? The copywriter and the usability engineer should be the best of friends within the development group. Both of their skill-sets are needed to help the site achieve its objectives. But how many senior writers are accorded the same respect that the usability engineer enjoys? How often do they work together as peers in an atmosphere of mutual respect?

A Brief History of Designers and Copywriters Online.

When it comes to influencing the form and function of a site, designers also have a big advantage over writers because of their closer kinship with programmers and usability engineers. Visit your local Web development company and you'll see the programmers and designers sitting together, looking at each other's work and getting along like a house on fire. Well, they may not always get along that well, but they have a lot more in common with each other than they do with copywriters.

Designers have that advantage over writers online because the designers have a much closer affinity with, and history of, working with sophisticated software. Go back to the mid-eighties and the arrival of the Mac and Page-Maker design software. Many designers were very quick to jump in to master this new design medium. As a result, they became very familiar with the use of computers, and more importantly, they figured out how to use some very complicated software. Many then went on to look at design within a multimedia environment. So when the time came to sit down with programmers and the usability people to build

Web pages, the designers took to it like ducks to water. They were ready for the Web.

Copywriters, as a whole, were not ready. While designers were working on their computer skills, most copywriters were content with the 10 percent of their word processing program that they actually used. Word processing software is a just a fancy replacement for a typewriter that allows you to correct all your mistakes without having to run out and buy more correction fluid. Copywriters have no real need for anything more sophisticated. So, when the Web arrived, copywriters just weren't there in the same space as the designers and programmers. They didn't get it, didn't see it coming, and weren't prepared to take on a whole new way of writing.

As a result, copywriters online often find themselves in a position that is junior to that of the designer. And if the designer is not sensitive to the need for great copy on the site, it becomes tough for the copywriter to do his or her job properly.

As just one example, a designer's influence can detract from the strength of the copy on a page when the copywriter is told that the copy is too long. Cut that copy! There are always plenty of compelling reasons why it's a great idea to cut the length of copy. Sometimes it's hard to resist. But every copywriter needs to resist cutting copy for the wrong reasons, because once people start gnawing away at the text, they won't stop until the text is down to almost nothing. The best description of this process can be found in Harold Evans's excellent book, *Editing and Design*. Here's the story:

> A fishmonger in England put up a sign that said FRESH FISH SOLD HERE. A friend suggests that he erase the word FRESH—because naturally the fish is fresh. No point in saying the obvious. Then he suggests removing the word HERE—for the same reasons. Of course it is "here." Next to go is the word SOLD—because it's not like the fish is being given away. And finally, he suggests removing the word FISH—because you can smell the store a mile away.

What's left? No words and no meaning. It's a facetious story but illustrates well how easy it is to come up with very good and defensible reasons for cutting words from someone's copy. Yes, copy can often be shortened and is often improved in the process. But there comes a point when any further reduction in length starts stripping away all meaning. And even if the meaning survives, the life and spirit of the message rarely survives excessive editing.

One More Thing: Make Peace with the Content Manager.

Copywriters online are generally not held in high regard by content managers. What are content managers? For those sites that employ them, they are the individuals responsible for all the words on a site. Their roles may change slightly from site to site, but they are usually part editor, part information architect, part writer. It's their job to ensure a high quality of writing across all aspects of the site. However, they are typically not marketers and many of them have a strong aversion to marketing text.

In the words of Amy Gahran of Contentious.com:

> I personally cringe when I hear about people looking for "copywriters" for their Web sites. That one little word says a lot—it means that the Web site is viewed as an advertisement, a brochure, a marketing campaign. In turn, that general mindset makes it more likely that pushing marketing messages will be a higher priority than simply meeting information needs.

She's right to be nervous about the arrival of a "copywriter" when that can signal the arrival of an offline writer with little understanding of, or sensitivity to, the online environment. But if her view is widely held within the industry, it can also represent a significant barrier to the writing of really good copy. If content managers are averse to copywriters, it's unlikely that they'll entertain new ways of writing that are more clearly aimed at driving user actions and increasing site conversion rates.

It's unfortunate that content managers, designers, and usability engineers appear to have arrived at their low opinions of copywriters by looking at the work of bad copywriters. There is a view that copywriters are all at the same level as the crass, rude salesperson at your local car dealership. Or that being a copywriter is somehow synonymous with the worst junk mail or those irritating phone calls from telemarketers. Good copywriters hate bad copy as much as anyone else:

> I have this heartfelt theory that people hate ads. Ads interrupt TV programmes and bulk out newspapers and mags and are generally a waste of perfectly good trees. So I try to avoid writing "ads." Or at least I try to make my stuff look different, so that it doesn't scream off the page "Hi! I'm an ad! Ignore me!"
>
> Neil French, Copywriter
>
> Source: *The Copywriter's Bible*, AD & AD Mastercraft Series.

Good copywriters (and Neil French is a *very* good copywriter) would agree with most of the views of content managers, Web designers, and usability engineers. There is very little distance between their opinions. They all hate cheap, intrusive advertising and marketing.

How to Catch Everyone's Attention.

The odds are stacked against copywriters being treated with equal respect on the development team right now. It's the way it is, and it will take time to change things. In the meantime, here are some ways to start opening the cracks.

First, recognize that others involved in Web development are not always being foolish in their suspicions of copywriters. Designers, usability engineers, and others recognize the unique nature of commerce online and are concerned by those writers who view it as just another advertising medium.

Second, for writers to become accepted on equal terms within development groups, they have to better understand both the different demands of writing online and the jobs and challenges of others on the team.

Third, copywriters need to do some great work and generate some measurable results. Sites live or die according to their conversion rates. Founders lose sleep and get up in the middle of the night to figure out what percentage of visitors are moving forward from the homepage, how many are signing up or subscribing, how many are putting items in the shopping cart, and how many of those people actually complete a purchase. These are key metrics that can spell success or failure for a business online.

For the copywriter, this is good news. Because at key points within a site or in an outbound email, it isn't too hard to make some small changes to text that will increase those conversion rates. Once you have the attention of your ultimate bosses, some of that new respect will—it is hoped—trickle down.

Time for a New Attitude within the Development Group.

The dotcom crash of 2000 and 2001 saw the end of the first era of marketing online. There were many brave attempts to leverage this new environment as a marketing medium. Most failed, and the few that survived have had to adjust their business models and their attitudes.

Some of that capacity for change also has to occur within development groups. Good copywriters need to be recognized and welcomed as key members of the inner team. To exclude them makes no sense. How can a commerce site survive within an environment as text-centric as the Net without the heavy influence of a writer? And how can a commerce site hope to increase its conversion rates and trade profitably without the input of a copywriter who can drive customer actions online?

Where is this next generation of great copywriters to be found? Some will have migrated from the offline advertising world, and others will be fresh from college and ready to start their copywriting careers online. But whatever their source, there is no sense in their arriving at your business if they are not valued, respected, and allowed to do their jobs.

CHAPTER THREE

ONLY WORDS WILL SET YOU APART

Set Your Company Apart Online

One of the most vexing challenges facing companies online is how to differentiate themselves from their many competitors. While this may be a problem for many companies fighting it out in the high street as well, it is a particular challenge for companies doing business on the Web.

There are several barriers to easy differentiation when marketing online. One of the most basic of these barriers is the limitation imposed by the hardware that your customers use. Whatever your business and whatever its size, your "canvas" will always be confined within the limits of your customers' computer monitors. In the offline world, large companies can differentiate themselves quite simply just by spending more. That's how customers know that some companies are bigger than others. Bigger stores. Bigger offices. Bigger ads. Bigger billboards. Online, size counts for nothing, because every company's Web site has to work within the same monitor size. The playing field, in that regard, is level.

Next comes the problem of bandwidth. The majority of users access the Web through a dial-up connection. This limits what you can reasonably deliver to that small monitor. It's not a TV. In short, large companies and small are all working within the same limitations. Your pages will look and behave in much the same way as those of a company that is either hundreds of times larger or hundreds of times smaller than your own. And if desktop monitor sizes make life hard, things get tougher still when you're presenting your company through the even smaller screens of a personal digital assistant (PDA) or cell phone. Three or four square inches give you very little space with which to differentiate your company.

Beyond the effects of hardware, the software that frames everyone's experience online also conspires to make everything appear the same. All emails, from IBM or from your best friend, arrive and are announced with the same short "From" and "Subject" lines. Flash intros on homepages play the same, tired dances. Requests for online help trigger the same, familiar pop-ups.

To make life even more complicated, there are compelling arguments for deliberately making your site the same as everyone else's from a usability standpoint. People find the Internet hard enough to use as it is. So it makes sense to keep the basic architecture and design of your site in line with those of your peers and competitors. Users like to know that they can look at the top or left side of your page to find the basic navigation links. They expect the familiarity of text that says, "Home," "About Us," and "Help." The more your site follows the most widely held conventions in design and architecture, the easier it will be for your customers to find their way around. And your customers are quite right to expect you to waste as little of their time as possible. Why should they spend their valuable time on figuring out how your site works?

Hardware, software, and usability considerations are all driving business online toward building sites that look and behave the same as everyone else's. But there is a very significant downside to this trend. The more you become like your competitors, the less able you are to differentiate your products and services. And if differentiation is a key marketing consideration in the offline world, it deserves even greater attention online.

Competing in a World of Too Many Choices.

Consumers are overwhelmed by choices. A large supermarket carries over 40,000 brand items on its shelves. In the United States, television viewers used to choose among three networks for their viewing choices: ABC, CBS, and NBC. Today, with cable and satellite in more and more homes, a wired household can choose between 150 or more channels. In the early seventies, McDonald's offered a choice of 13 items for your fast-food pleasure. By the late nineties it offered 43.

More choices lead to more competition, which, in turn, leads to the need for more advertising. Today it is estimated that the average American is exposed to more than 3,000 separate advertising messages a day. That's over a million messages a year. It's overwhelming.

In his book *Differentiate or Die,* Jack Trout quotes consumer psychologist Carol Moog as saying:

> Too many choices, all of which can be fulfilled instantly, indulged immediately, keeps children—and adults—infantile. From a marketing perspective, people stop caring, get as fat and fatigued as foie gras geese, and lose their decision-making capabilities. They withdraw and protect against the overstimulation; they get "bored."

When these overstimulated and bored consumers arrive online, they are simply jumping out of the frying pan and into the fire. According to eMarketer, a leading supplier of Internet statistics, there were more than 6 million active Web sites out there by 2001. The search engine Google is just scratching the surface of those sites when it indexes over 1.3 billion pages. As a result, consumers are faced with an impossible number of choices. Where should they go for the products and services they are looking for? Which sites should they trust? Which names can they depend on?

For consumers these are tough questions. At least at the mall they can judge a store quickly by its appearance. But online, with most stores looking more or less the same, consumers have very few clues to work with. Recognizing this, during the late nineties many online retail sites took some pretty desperate measures in largely failed attempts to differentiate themselves. One example that jumps quickly to mind is the Boo.com retail store. The site designers and programmers added just about every fancy bell and whistle that they could. Yes, they differentiated their site from all others. But in doing so, they made it almost impossible for their visitors to make a purchase. The site was just too complicated. Another popular trick used by desperate online sites was to reduce prices and try to undercut their competitors. It was a classic move that ultimately proved self-destructive for thousands of ecommerce sites as they quickly ran out of money. If a business online cannot reasonably differentiate itself with its technology, its design, or its prices, what can it do to separate itself from the competition?

Only Words Will Set You Apart.

Words can set you apart with the lightest of touches. In the same way that the people you know have unique ways of expressing themselves with words, so too can businesses online. And the beauty of words online is that their simplicity allows for an infinite variety of expression.

When it comes to communications, words are the simplest and most effective of tools. The benefits of a simple tool are beautifully expressed by William Gibson in his novel *All Tomorrow's Parties*:

> The handles of a craftsman's tools bespeak an absolute simplicity, the plainest forms affording the greatest range of possibilities for the user's hand.
>
> That which is overdesigned, too highly specific, anticipates outcome; the anticipation of outcome guarantees, if not failure, the absence of grace.

He was talking about a knife, one of the simplest of all tools. But he could just as well have been talking about words.

Simplicity of language does afford a great range of possibilities. You can do what you want with words. You're not tied to a particular software platform. Words don't care which browser your customers use. Words are the ultimate open-source code for communication. Everyone uses them, and the "language" they build evolves daily to reflect the shifts and changes in our cultures.

By contrast, "that which is overdesigned" limits our choices. Desktop publishing software is overdesigned, as is Web design software and customer relationship management (CRM) software. The options and horizons they offer are all limited by the vision and imagination of their creators. The outcomes you can achieve have been anticipated by the people who wrote the code. To paraphrase William Gibson, something that is overdesigned anticipates the outcome. And when the outcome is anticipated, it is limited—and everything begins to look the same.

The absolute simplicity of words offers the only lasting solution when it comes to setting yourself apart from the competition.

Great Copy Has Always
Differentiated Companies.

It has often been the job of the copywriter to sit down and do the hard thinking when it comes to setting the client apart from its competitors. For the most part, the results may fall a little short. If writing great copy were easy, getting it right wouldn't be so effective when it is achieved. But from time to time a talented writer will demonstrate just how effectively some carefully crafted words can make a difference—and how a good copywriter is also a natural born marketer. Here are a few such words from one of America's greatest copywriters, Bill Bernbach.

For Volkswagen:

Think small.

For Levy's Jewish rye bread:

You don't have to be Jewish to enjoy Levy's Jewish rye bread.

For Avis:

Because we're only number two in rent-a-cars, we try harder.

This last one turned the Avis underdog into a powerhouse in the industry.

It took a few years before another great copywriter, Jim Durfee, wrote a series of powerful headlines for the company that was number one, Hertz. Here's one of them:

No.2 says he tried harder. Than who?

He neatly cut the legs out from under the Avis campaign. Headlines like these demonstrate the tremendous power of just a few words when it comes to altering people's perceptions of your company.

Arguably, you won't find as many great writers in the offline world as you did a couple of decades ago. Or more accurately, you won't find writers being trained as well, nourished as enthusiastically, or rewarded as highly. You get what you deserve. So if you want great writing, you'd better invest in it.

Of course, great headlines can also just fall in your lap. One of the most famous headlines for Volkswagen was the single word, "lemon." It wasn't the copywriter or art director assigned to the job who came up with that. The story goes that it was another writer, Rita Selden, who happened by their office, saw the ad in progress, and suggested the one-word headline. Does this mean that writing great lines is easy? Not at all. That happy accident would never have taken place if all the people involved weren't enormously talented and if they hadn't been open and receptive to great suggestions, whatever their source.

On the Web, words can set your site apart just as economically and just as powerfully. Right now, that kind of powerful writing just isn't happening. The dominance of technological "solutions" casts such a huge shadow over every aspect of commerce online, nobody is paying enough attention to the power of a few carefully chosen words.

A Brief, Academic Aside...

For anyone who thinks there is a limit to what can be said briefly and simply with just a few words, here's an interesting piece of math from Steven Pinker, professor in the Department of Brain and Cognitive Sciences at MIT:

> Say everyday English has four determiners (*a, any, one,* and *the*) and ten thousand nouns. Then the rule for a noun phrase allows four choices for the determiner, followed by ten thousand choices for the head noun, yielding $4 \times 10,000 = 40,000$ ways to utter a noun phrase. The rule for a sentence allows these forty thousand subjects to be followed by any of four thousand verbs, providing $40,000 \times 4,000 = 160,000,000$ ways to utter the first three words of a sentence. Then there are four choices for the

determiner of the object (640 million four-word beginnings) followed by ten thousand choices for the head noun of the object, or 640,000,000 × 10,000 = 6,400,000,000,000 (6.4 trillion) five-word sentences. Suppose it takes five seconds to produce one of these sentences. To crank them all out, from *The abandonment abased the abbey* and *The abandonment abased the abbot,* through *The abandonment abased the zoologist,* all the way to *The zoologist zoned the zoo,* would take a million years.

True, not every combination could usefully find its way into your next page rewrite or outbound email. But if you have 6.4 trillion choices with just five words, there's no excuse for pumping out the same old tired text every time you put keyboard to paper. There's no need to sound just like everyone else, and there are compelling business reasons not to.

A Unique Voice Differentiates and Is Defensible.

Here are three examples of welcome messages from leading Web sites. This is the message someone receives immediately after signing up at these sites for the first time:

Welcome to Walmart.com! Thank you for becoming a registered user of our Web site. We appreciate your business and want to make your online shopping experience fast, easy and fun.

WELCOME to QVC's E-MAIL SERVICES. We're delighted that you've decided to take advantage of the speed and convenience of QVC e-mail communications.

Welcome to Victoria's Secret E-mail—exclusive e-mail news! Now that you have signed up to receive our special mailings, you'll be the first to hear about exciting new fashion and media events, special online promotions and more.

These messages aren't identical, but they are all very similar. The problem here is not that they all say the same kind of thing, but that they all sound as if they were written by the same person, sitting at the same desk at Welcome Emails-R-Us. Are Wal-Mart, QVC, and Victoria's Secret all the same? Do their brands all fit in the same space for you? Is it a matter of indifference to you whether you buy your lingerie from aisle 6 at Wal-Mart or from Victoria's Secret? If these companies' names and brands are so different, why do their emails sound the same? The simple answer is that nobody is paying close enough attention to how copy can be used to support and differentiate brands and companies online.

This lack of attention represents a huge wasted opportunity. By way of contrast, here's the welcome text from a site called Customatix. Customatix enables you to design and build your own athletic shoes online, and its welcome email reflects the company's unique position in the marketplace:

> **Well, you've done it now. By opening a Customatix account, you've just changed the way you're going to buy athletic shoes forever. Be careful. The surgeon general reports that designing your own cool athletic shoes can be highly addictive.**

Unlike the Victoria's Secret message, this one speaks volumes about the character and style of the company. This didn't come off the printer at Welcome Emails-R-Us. The voice is unique and fits perfectly with the site and its services. But is it perhaps too cool and chatty, at the expense of being effective? Not at all. It clearly identifies the services offered at the site and continues the sales process by making the prospect of designing athletic shoes sound incredibly attractive. The company has simply taken the trouble to think carefully about the text and how to make this email count. The Customatix email adds to and supports its brand, while the vanilla-style Victoria's Secret email diminishes and dilutes its brand.

Not only do words do a great job of differentiating your business online, but they do so in a way that is highly defensible. When you give your site a unique character by using a voice that is unmistakably yours, you also insulate your business from your competitors. This isn't the case with technology or pricing. If you offer online live help on Monday, your competition can do the same by Friday. If you decide to show your products in three dimensions this month, your competitors can do the same next month. If you cut your prices by 20 percent this morning, they can cut theirs by 25 percent this afternoon. Competition online is on steroids. Changes happen fast. So there's little point in investing in changes that are designed to differentiate your business if those changes can be copied within just a few hours, days, or weeks. Better to invest in words—because when you build a unique character with words, you have something that's much harder to take away.

Work with a Voice That Has Strong Character.

If you're a bricks-and-mortar company coming to the Web, you're at a significant disadvantage when it comes to creating a strong online voice. In the offline world, companies are very careful about how they present themselves to the world. Too many years of focus groups, demographic research results, and nail-biting caution have resulted in companies' taking the safe route, most of the time. This is certainly true in their offline advertising efforts. It's a very brave company that would take the risk of being seen as silly, frivolous, or foolish in the public eye. But online, those same circumstances and rules don't necessarily apply.

Take the case of The Motley Fool at Fool.com. This is a company that makes a deliberate policy of appearing foolish. Here's how it describes itself:

What Is The Motley Fool?

The Motley Fool was founded in 1993 by brothers David and Tom Gardner. Our name derives from Elizabethan drama, where only the court jester (the "Fool") could tell the King the truth without getting his head lopped off. We're dedicated to educating, amusing, and enriching individuals in search of the truth.

What Is the Truth?

The stark truth is that the financial world preys on ignorance and fear. But now, gentle reader, you've set your virtual feet on Foolish soil and your days of fear and intimidation are over. We exist to serve you, to teach you, and to have a heck of a lot of fun along the way. The Fool is a highly collaborative forum, and we do have a few rules of the road. What follows is a disclaimer that the lawyers made us write, but one that's aimed to protect you as much as it does our humble enterprise. So hoist the flags! Cue the fanfare! It's time to read. . .

The voice of this company is not only different; it is strong and unmistakable. The company has a unique character that it developed online and has since managed to apply to a newspaper column, a radio show, and a series of books.

But it probably couldn't have grown its business in this way if it had started out offline. Had it started out with its "foolish" ways from a mall location, nobody would have taken the company seriously. People who talk about investments aren't meant to talk or behave like that. But The Motley Fool can and has succeeded online. Why? Because the Internet was built on and thrives on the strong voices of its participants. Online you need to have a strong character in order to stand out from the crowd. The Net is a vast community of voices—articulate, witty, ridiculous, and loud. So character counts for something. Being blah guarantees that you'll never be heard.

The mistake many businesses make online is that they display the same caution as they do in the offline world. The result is that they appear to be completely characterless. It's a little like that person at a party who always tries to fit in, always tries to take on the characteristics of those around him, always tries be one of the guys. Individuals like that tend not to get a great deal of respect. Better to be known for your strong beliefs, your unique personality. Better to be hated by some than ignored by everyone. Or in the words of British author Kingsley Amis:

> If you can't annoy somebody, there is little point in writing.

Unfortunately, very few companies take the plunge, tap into the unique character of their company, and use language to communicate their particular voice.

A Human Voice Is Always Reassuring.

A unique voice on your site and within your emails not only differentiates you from everyone else out there but is also very reassuring to your users. The Web is an astonishing construct of various technologies and, for all its wonders, can be a very cold and unforgiving place. This is particularly true if your visitors are new to computers and the Web. Before you shrug and assume that you have a hugely sophisticated audience, this is very likely not the case. Most Web users are relatively new to the Web, and many of them are new to working with PCs and having one in their home. If you take the cautious view and assume that many of your existing and prospective customers are fairly new to all of this, you might find that the addition of a human voice to your site would go a long way to calming the fears or concerns of your customers.

In the case of one site that has made a business of targeting newbies on the Web, the voice of its founders on the homepage is integral to its approach:

**"Welcome To
The Newbie Club™"**

Hi, this is Tom Glander and Joe Robson, the two crazy co-founders of the most talked about and most respected Newbie-learning site on the Web. . . Are you sick to death of Techies and mystifying "Tutorials" spouting four letter words like byte and frag, JPEG and JAVA and other jargonistic gobbledygook? Wouldn't you like to know how to make your PC do exactly what **you** want it to do? To stop it acting like it has a mind of its own, and just let you enjoy yourself for a change?

How would you like to use the Internet without fear of getting lost and confused? To confidently send email in a flash, and even build your own Family or Business webpages? Because you can you know—you **really** can.

First, the site founders introduce themselves, and then they do something that real people do but that marketing copy often doesn't; they ask questions. Yes, the introduction is self-serving and the questions are leading, but that's OK. What they achieve by adding a human voice to the page is to create a connection point with their users. You don't have to understand the navigation etiquette of the Web to get started on this page. You can simply do what you'd do with a sheet of paper—just start reading.

There is a temptation to cut back as much text as possible, particularly on a homepage. The homepage "real estate" is considered too valuable by many to accommodate long text. But perhaps they're wrong. Perhaps the homepage is the perfect spot for some longer text. Perhaps this is where you can allow your voice to sing out from the page as a warm and unique welcome to your visitors, new and old. It's a great way to connect with your users and a simple way to separate yourself from your competitors.

A Unified Voice Doesn't Happen by Accident.

If you want to create a unique voice that is heard by all your customers on a consistent basis, across all channels, you have to work on making it happen. The more personal your company voice becomes, the greater the challenge to keep it sounding the same across multiple channels and media. It's easy with "corporate-speak," because everyone in the organization can learn the same, lifeless, vanilla style from the same company handbook. That's the attraction of corporate-speak. But if you want to set yourself apart with a voice and a style that differentiates your company from all its competitors, you're going to have to work very hard to make that voice part of your corporate culture.

Cynthia Currence is national vice president of Strategic Marketing & Branding, for the American Cancer Society and is very aware of the challenge such a large organization faces when protecting its voice and its brand. ACS is a huge organization with 97 percent name recognition in the United States and over 2 million volunteers across the country. Within that organization, Cynthia Currence describes how keeping the voice consistent happens only when you plan for it and train for it:

> We identified four brand values that are the pillars of the American Cancer Society experience. This has helped us develop a spirit of accuracy and informed decision-making. It has also helped our many internal audiences—our staff, our volunteers, those who believe in us and love us—to understand what psychological and emotional space to leave people in.
>
> Our communication scenario is widely distributed, with about 2 million volunteers, all of whom are very passionate spokespeople about the issue of cancer and about the American Cancer Society. So for years we have had an opportunity to explore ways to make sure that people understand what is accurate, what is true and what is a good reflection of the American Cancer Society as a brand.
>
> Training is a critical element—making sure that people go to some sort of centralized training or that the curriculum for that training has been developed and then diffused through the orga-

nization. If you don't have adequate training, and regular training, there is very little hope that you can stay on top of it. We have a wonderful communications process put in place by our corporate communications department which sends out field notices on a regular basis. So our staff across the country know if something new is coming up, and how you position this and answer questions relevant to it. We also have quarterly trainings for our marketing communications people where we take a look at things that are emerging or coming on the horizon—again, to try to make sure that we are all in the same place at the same time.

ACS is an interesting example to look at because, as a nonprofit organization, its mission is based entirely around serving the needs of its constituents. It needs to stand out from competing nonprofits, and it needs its public to view it as the primary and most trusted source of information on cancer. As a result, ACS has developed a very impressive and deep expertise in the area of brand and voice development. Many for-profit companies, both offline and online, could learn a lot from understanding how large an investment in research and training it takes to have your company speak with one, unified voice.

You Need Skilled Copywriters.

It's simple to write ordinary copy that sets your site side by side with dozens of other, ordinary competitors. But to create copy that sets you apart, it takes a great deal more skill. You need to employ and train copywriters who can create a unique voice and character for your site. You need to give those copywriters the authority to apply that voice across all channels and media. And you need to make sure that as the voice develops over time, its message and its tone remain consistent with your company vision.

CHAPTER FOUR

THE VELOCITY OF WORDS

Use the Velocity of Words to Spread Your Message

Words have tremendous, natural velocity online. Email, instant messaging, discussion lists, and forums all allow for written words to travel between individuals at a speed and frequency that was simply unimaginable in the days before the Web. When it comes to spreading the written word, nothing facilitates fast travel better than the Web.

Here's a story that illustrates just how quickly a few words can travel online. In the spring of 1996 a group of college freshmen were throwing a ball around in a hallway and broke the glass on an emergency exit sign. They cleaned up the glass and then, for some weird reason, wrote the following slogan on the sign:

Mr T Ate My Balls.

From then on, all these guys started saying "Mr T ate my balls" at the slightest provocation. It just became a funny thing to say. Next thing you know, everyone is saying it. Then one of the people in that hallway, Nehal Patel, built the Mr T Ate My Balls Web site. The site included pictures of Mr T from the TV show delivering such memorable lines as, "Gimme your balls, fool!" To date, that site has received over a million visitors. Next stop was the Chewbacca Ate My Balls! site. That opened the doors to dozens of other people creating their own sites, from Ronald Reagan Ate My Balls! to Pokemon Ate My Balls! The Ate My Balls Web ring soon included over 300 individual sites.

That's pretty impressive distribution for a few words of pure nonsense. And it illustrates very well how a saying can come out of nowhere and use the Web to spread out and be seen by millions. Remember Mahir Cagri? Probably not. When his Web site went up in 1999, showing Mahir in a red Speedo and playing the accordion, this unknown Turk enjoyed a brief moment of fame around the world. Was it the red Speedo? No. It was the three words that jumped out of his amateur homepage.

I KISS YOU!!!!!

With these three words he became an almost instant celebrity. Why? Who knows. But words have a way of finding a niche in our brains and then demanding to be shared with others. It just takes the right word or phrase being uttered at the right time in the right context. However, one thing is pretty consistent across all the sayings that spread around the country or world with such astonishing velocity. These catchphrases are short, usually five words or less. That seems to be the limit when it comes to smooth and fast distribution.

Of course, in the wake of "I KISS YOU," the statement "I LOVE YOU" was a natural carrier for one of the most damaging viruses ever spread over the Internet. By the end of May 2000, the "I LOVE YOU" virus had caused hundreds of millions of dollars' worth of damage around the world. By traveling through the Outlook contact files on susceptible computers, the virus spread with amazing speed. But why did so many people open the file and let the virus free on their computer? Because of the words "I LOVE YOU." Several reports at the time spoke of people in offices expressing disappointment when they didn't receive the virus. Did they really want their computers infected? No, but they did want to feel loved.

Hollywood Understands Velocity.

If you're racking your brain for examples of short statements with big velocity, think about the movies and TV.

Show me the money!

I see dead people.

Is that your final answer?

You had me at hello.

Astalavista, baby.

Danger, Will Robinson!

Shagadelic!

One entertainment company that has clearly understood the natural velocity of words is New Line Cinema. New Line Cinema is home to the people who brought us the Austin Powers movies. The first movie grossed $56.4 million at the box office and cost less than $10 million to produce. A pretty good return on investment. But it was after the movie was released on video that the real magic started to happen. It caught fire in the video markets because hundreds of thousands of people were standing around in school halls and office cubicles saying, "Yeah baby!" and "Shagadelic!"

Gordon Paddison, senior vice president at New Line Cinema, remembers how the company used "Austin Speak" to get people talking:

> Particular pop culture "Austin Speak" catch phrases were used to position the film, and included to punctuate the TV campaign, which reinforced the character and the association.

Did New Line Cinema then cancel its advertising budget because word of mouth was doing all the heavy lifting for it? Not at all. But it did ride the wave. When the time came to start promoting the second movie, online banner ads were used to further seed the market with the words and phrases that had proved so popular from the first movie. Movie fans were then happy to spread the word further through email and instant messaging. People were enthusiastic about spreading the word, not only because they liked the Austin Powers movie, but also because they liked repeating those words and phrases. Yeah, baby!

The Velocity of Words Moves Products.

Copywriters on Madison Avenue, and in other clusters of advertising agencies around the world, rack their brains to come up with great phrases that will capture the imaginations of millions of consumers.

Got milk?

Where's the Beef?

The real thing.

Whassup?

We try harder.

Just do it.

Of course, there are thousands of other advertising slogans that are resoundingly unsuccessful and disappear without a trace as soon as the ad budget runs dry. But when sayings catch fire, spread fast, and endure in the public mind, the companies behind them reap tremendous rewards. The viral nature of the message, and the way in which it endures, helps secure a huge amount of added value from every marketing dollar spent. However, to make the velocity of words work for you online, you need to get a few things right.

First, you need to have something worth talking about. People aren't going to open up their instant messaging software and start chatting with everyone they know just because you've introduced a new soap powder. Self-delusion is probably the number one cause of the failure of most word-of-mouth marketing efforts. Marketers sit around a desk and somehow persuade themselves that the saying they dreamed up for their product or service is so exciting that people are going to trip over themselves in their excitement to tell the world.

The sad truth is, very few products or services are that exciting. Free email from Hotmail was. ICQ instant messaging was. But how many other services or physical products online can you think of that have "gone viral"? And even if you do have a hugely compelling product, what are the chances that you'll come up with a short catchphrase that will help spread the word?

Unless you are about to launch the new Hotmail, put aside the notion that you can use word-of-mouth marketing in the place of paid-for advertising. Instead, start thinking about how you can use word-of-mouth to make every advertising dollar work a whole lot harder.

Setting Reasonable Expectations.

It's a noble ambition to seek out the next advertising phrase that will pass into the catchphrase hall of fame.

Keep at it. But in the meantime, there are ways in which you can tap into the natural velocity of words at a more practical level.

First, your customers love to chat about the products and services they buy. These conversations used to be confined to places where friends, neighbors, and colleagues would gather together and have a few moments to talk. Now, of course, these conversations take place online. The groups are larger, and the volume of words shared is phenomenal. According to a year 2000 study by eMarketer:

> 12 billion text messages are sent globally every month. 9 billion come from PCs, personal digital assistants and mobile phones, and the other 3 billion come from pagers.

Twelve billion is a very big number. That's a lot of words flying between millions of people around the world every single month. It's here, within the collective voice of millions of prospects and customers, that you can get a feel for the kind of language that has velocity. You can find out which terms and phrases are current and which are proving to be popular. Based on what you learn, you'll be in a better position to write the kind of copy for your site and emails that taps into the natural language of your audience online. Unless you're a top copywriter working for a huge brand name, you probably won't get to be famous as the author of a five-word tag line that travels the planet. But you will be able to tap into the natural velocity of words within the online environment.

For instance, if you were writing Web pages or emails promoting the new Volkswagen Beetle, you might want to check out what enthusiasts are saying at Topica.com, one of the major online destinations for newsletters and discussion groups. After a few minutes you'll get a pretty good sense that these people truly love their cars.

The New Beetle is far more than just a car. We NB owners are a special breed, and the NB community is an amazing group. I feel honored and privileged to be a part of it.

Dig a little deeper and you'll see that people name their VW Bugs and even celebrate the cars' birthdays. Here are a few of the more interesting names people have chosen for their Beetles:

StudBug

Spacepod

Podkayne

CiaoBug

RoseBug

Scarab

You get the idea. These people get pretty excited by their cars. So if you were writing emails or newsletters for VW Beetle owners, you'd have a tremendous opportunity to tap into that excitement. After reading a few dozen posts, you'll get a feel for the kind of language these owners use. You could even start working on newsletter titles, competitions, and events that would tap into the owners' interest in naming and celebrating their cars. And if you try out a number of phrases that you think might catch that group's imagination, you could see some tremendous velocity at work as a popular phrase travels the network. Perhaps something as simple as a competition—the NewBug Birthday competition—could get people talking about NewBug birthdays. You'll never know until you try, and you may have to present 50 different phrases until one catches on and works for you. But even if you don't come up with a nifty phrase, you should obsess about what your customers are saying and how they are saying it. This will give you invaluable insight into how best to phrase and present your own marketing copy. Take advantage of the fact that the Internet is a shared space and allow your customers to become participants in the formation of your promotional messages. The more they are involved, the more they will feel ownership of what's being said and the more likely they are to spread the word.

In some instances, much of the writing for a company's site is quite literally written by the site's visitors or members. Smallbusiness.com is a site aimed, predictably, at small-business people, and its content is created by its own users. Small-business people write and post their advice, recommendations, and experiences on the site so that others can learn from their triumphs, their failures, and their expertise. The business people who post the advice get a moment of fame and sometimes some new business through the exposure they get at the site. The people who read the advice get to participate by both delving into and rating the advice from a very deep well of knowledge.

When you read the copy written by the creators of the Smallbusiness.com site, or the emails they send out, you get a very strong sense that the voice of the company is very much in tune with the voices and attitudes of the contributors. It's not that the site behaves like a chameleon, constantly trying to be hip to the latest voices on the site, but it does manage to maintain a voice that definitely fits the culture. Here's an opening from one of the emails it sends out to its members:

Dear John Smith

We've just launched the smallbusiness.com Directory! (Insert wild applause and cheering)

Already, our directory includes listings for more than 100,000 small businesses spanning 9,000 categories. These numbers are growing every day, most likely because a) basic directory listings are free and b) we have lots of friends. But mostly it's because of (a).

The email has a conversational tone and a tongue-in-cheek quality that works well to break down any distance between the writer and the audience. The joke is shared, and the language of the email is of a tone that can easily be found within member posts on the site.

When you write in a way that is both true to your own vision and also responsive to the language of your audience, special things start to happen. Your audience members feel good. They feel like they have a personal stake in what's happening. And when people really feel they have a personal stake in something, they like to share. They like to tell their friends and say, one way or another, "Hey, look what I'm part of! You should join up too!"

Encourage Velocity with "Tell a Friend."

In common with many sites, Smallbusiness.com has a link and a form that enables visitors to email a page from the site to their friends and colleagues. "Tell a friend" systems are a very smooth way in which to spread the word about your site. Best of all, the words being spread are not your own, but those of your users. What's so great about that? It's great because the words of your satisfied users carry more weight and credibility than yours would. If you, the site owner, send a stranger an email about how great your site is, it's spam. When one of your members sends the same person a link to your site, along with some words of praise, it's an act of friendship.

The most important part of the "Tell a friend" page is the field in which the sender is invited to add a short message. It's tempting to write this message yourself. After all, as the writer or marketing person at your site, you certainly know how best to articulate the key benefits of the site. But this is one of those rare occasions when you'd do well to keep those typing fingers away from the keyboard. When a "Tell a friend" recommendation arrives in the voice of the site owners, the words lose both credibility and velocity in a real hurry. Here's an example of an email that was generated by a "Tell a friend" form:

> Welcome to AccuWeather.com! This message has been generated by the AccuWeather Automatic Email Get-The-Word-Out Form (tm). An aquaintance of yours, one [your name will be placed here], has discovered the coolest, hippest, MOST ACCURATE weather on the web at AccuWeather.com, and wants you to join in the fun!
>
> And please, after you visit let us know what you think! [your name will be placed here] was impressed, and we think you will be too!
>
> Best Regards,
> The AccuWeather.com Development Team

Imagine that Jack, a 50-year-old potato farmer in Idaho, wants his cousin, Frank, in Texas, to know about AccuWeather.com. What is Frank going to think when he reads this:

> Jack has discovered the coolest, hippest, MOST ACCURATE weather on the web at AccuWeather.com, and wants you to join in the fun!

Does this sound like the kind of language that Jack would use or that Frank would believe? Does the "Development Team" really believe that this is how everyone talks?

You're better off leaving the form blank and allowing people to write in their own words. Let Jack say:

> Frank,
>
> I know you've been cursing for years about the wretched forecasts you get down there. So before you blame another poor

54

harvest on the local weatherman, I thought you might like to join the twenty-first century and follow the weather on the Internet.

Give my best to Susan and the boys.

Jack

You may not be able to predict or control what people say when you leave the form blank, but at least the sincerity of their voices will be recognized and welcomed by the final recipients.

Humor Gets People Clicking.

Most business communications lack humor. Most emails, newsletters, and Web pages fail to break away from the assumption that all marketing has to be serious. On TV, on radio, and in print you might find humor being used from time to time. But not too often, as a humorous approach is often viewed as being too risky.

Online, it makes sense to be a little more open to using humor in your communications, because it is hugely viral in nature. MeMail.com describes itself as "an electronic magazine rack" and publishes dozens of different online publications. One of its most popular newsletters is the Joke of the Day. As Kevin Needham, COO, observes, humor travels fast:

> Our humourous publications are the most viral content we put out there. Subscribers to the joke newsletters are not the most responsive readers when it came to selling them things—ecommerce products—but everyone likes their humour and each person would pass the joke on to 5 or 6 of their friends.

Just about everyone online must have received a joke from a friend through email at some point or another. Humor is something people like to share. It makes people feel good. Of course, this doesn't mean that every online communication should be accompanied by a joke, but it does mean that adding an element of humor can increase pass-along.

A site aimed at webmasters of small to medium-sized sites, Forkinthehead.com, once used its newsletter to run a competition among its readers. (*Disclaimer:* The author was a founder of Forkinthehead.com, but is no longer involved with the site or the company.) Participants had to write a limerick that had some connection with the business of building good Web sites, but it also had to include at least one reference to the word "fork." Here's one of the entries:

O Fork, you inspire deep dread

How many poor souls have you bled?

Yes, a website should work

But, dear Fork, must you lurk

Then savagely lodge in my head?

Jim Rosenberg

It may not be side-splittingly funny, but it is amusing. Dozens of competitors not only sent in their own limericks, but also told their friends about it. The site wasn't about jokes, but it was about building community. A touch of humor proved to be a good way to spread the word.

Your Users' Own Words Have Great Velocity.

"Telling a friend" is just one way to tap into the enormous energy that drives communications between individuals online. Individuals may not be that interested in hearing from companies, but they are always interested in hearing from their friends, peers, and other people with similar interests. This interest in others who have some kind of connection with you is what lies behind the most important words on the Amazon.com Web site:

Customers who bought this book also bought:

When it comes to cross-selling, Amazon doesn't tell you what its staff think you should buy; it tells you what other people like you have chosen. Amazon follows those recommendations with reviews of the book you're looking at right now. And most of those reviews are written not by the publisher, but by Amazon.com customers. Amazon gains credibility by leaving the promotion of individual titles to the marketplace itself. Amazon doesn't need to write and update hundreds of thousands of pages of content; it lets its customers do it. In fact, you can get a pretty good feel for the success or otherwise of a title simply by seeing how many customer reviews it has attracted.

The words of your customers have a lot more natural velocity than the words you write in-house. For one thing, as soon as someone writes a review at Amazon.com, a little extra buzz kicks in. That person may feel excited to see his review on the site and will likely tell his friends and colleagues to check it out. Or an acquaintance from thousands of miles away might stumble across the review and say to her friends, "Hey, I know the guy who wrote that. He's a good guy."

The same goes for sites like Epinions.com. Individuals can sign up and become reviewers for a huge range of products and services. Once again, as soon as you have a customer's name and photo up on the site, that buzz begins to happen again. You can count on the fact that the customer will be sending the URL to both friends and family.

The words of your customers have greater velocity than your own for a number of reasons. First, your customers have an immediate network of friends and family to which you have no access. So what they say on your site will, it is hoped, start to travel out almost immediately. Second, even strangers will probably feel more at ease with the opinion of another customer than with the "opinion" of your marketing department. Rightly or wrongly, there will be a sense that another customer can be better trusted. Third, the language used by your customers will probably be more "aerodynamic," with more natural velocity. Your customers speak like the real people they are, not like a marketing department that is hamstrung by bad habits or an overenthusiastic legal department.

As an example of the increased, natural velocity of your customers' voices, here's what Apple says about its 2001 Titanium laptop:

> It's a paradigm shift with profound implications for mobile professionals: the first supercomputer you can actually take with you on an airplane. Apart from being able to watch DVD movies on a stunning 15.2-inch (measured diagonally) widescreen format display with 1152×768-pixel resolution in millions of colors, just imagine being able to carry around the kind of horsepower you've previously associated only with systems like the Power Mac G4. That's exactly the advantage you get with the PowerBook G4.

While you're mulling over the meaning of "a paradigm shift with profound implications," take a look at what one of the reviewers at Epinions.com said about the same machine:

> Well, despite my numerous protests, my girlfriend went and bought a laptop computer. "Don't do that—a desktop is much cheaper! You'll be able to get more for much less!", I said in vain. When I found out she was not only buying a laptop, but a Mac, I was in real disgust. Being a Windows addict, I always found the Mac OS to be unnecessarily complicated and limited.

But well, nothing I said could prevent her from making this purchase. Just as recently as last week she received her new "baby."

I must say, to this day I kind of had to keep my mouth shut. . . I've never ever seen anything so tiny: this computer weighs a mere 5 pounds and it's only an inch thin! Despite these minimalistic features, it has a HUGE 15" wide screen.

His rave about the machine continues on for a few more paragraphs. The crucial difference with his text is that he was clearly talking from his heart and not from the marketing manual. He writes and thinks like regular people, not like regular marketers. As a result, his words are likely to resonate and connect far better with other people who are thinking of buying this machine.

Velocity comes through honesty, through feeling, through capturing the heart of the message in natural language. There are times when that voice can come directly from your customers, and there are other times when that voice will have to originate from your company.

Dead Prose Has No Velocity.

A key to maximizing the velocity of words is to be genuine and enthusiastic about what you're saying. The members of that online group of VW Bug owners were clearly excited about their cars and delighted to be able to share that enthusiasm with other Bug owners. People love to be part of high-energy groups with a shared passion. And passion can quickly become contagious.

The contagious nature of positive energy and good feelings is apparent all around us. Groups of happy kids in a playground make us smile. Wildly energetic pop stars with big smiles energize us. A happy face at a toll booth or gas pump can make our day. And those email jokes that find their way into millions of inboxes every day of the year lighten the moment with a laugh. People like to share jokes and good news. They like to feel good. They are even prepared to receive malicious viruses when they're accompanied by the words "I LOVE YOU!" Keep that in mind as you write. If you have customers who are genuinely enthusiastic about your products or services, immerse yourself in their feedback and discussion list posts. Feel your way into their language. Get a genuine sense of what is driving their feelings. What is it about your products that really turns people on? And what are the common threads and phrases that you find in your customers' language?

The genuine excitement of your customers carries tremendous velocity. Learn from that, and use it.

CHAPTER FIVE

WORDS BUILD RELATIONSHIPS

Create Lasting Relationships with Copy

For many businesses online, the prospect of creating lasting relationships with their customers is the Holy Grail. The argument is that developing a relationship with each customer one-on-one is more likely to result in keeping that customer for a longer period of time. In addition, a good relationship better insulates you from the predatory efforts of your competitors. Hence, the wide acceptance of relationship marketing and customer relationship management (CRM).

This premise makes a great deal of sense. However, the manner in which marketers set out to create these relationships raises some interesting questions. One of the core activities that companies pursue is the collection of information about customers in the belief that the better they know each customer and prospect, the more likely they are to build a lasting relationship. They'll collect demographic data so that they can "see" the customer more clearly. And they'll collect behavioral data so that they can track what those customers actually do and don't do while online. There's some incomplete, if not flawed, thinking here. Yes, collecting data about your customers and their behavior at your site may well increase the chances of your making more sales, if you act on that new knowledge effectively. But the collection of data itself does nothing to create a relationship. The collection of customer information is a one-way process, and the creation of a relationship is not. This approach brings to mind the picture of a young man trying to create a relationship with a young woman by finding out as much about her as possible. He might, if he were a little disturbed, go so far as to hire someone to compile a complete report on this woman's life and daily habits. If he then met her in a bar and used the knowledge he had gained, he could very well be in a strong position to capture her attention and interest. But would he be in a better position to create a lasting relationship? Probably not. Relationships are not built on data points. In fact, the collection of data in the absence of a relationship is somewhat creepy.

Can a relationship between a company and a customer develop once those data have been used to instigate a sale? Yes it can, so long as your customers have a good experience while purchasing your products or services and are satisfied with their purchases once they receive them. However, the collection and use of data alone should not be confused with the process of developing relationships. These are two different issues and should be addressed separately.

Think of it this way. The technology you use and the data you collect take you right up to the moment when you open your virtual mouth and start communicating with your prospects and customers. You have the extra knowledge to say all the right things. But what if you're a terrible communicator? What if you're the corporate equivalent of a tongue-tied teenager? If right at that end point, at the moment when you have to use your knowledge to build a relationship with your prospect, you do a bad job, then everything that came before is wasted. All the software in the world won't help you build strong relationships if you don't know how to talk and listen to your audience. The key is not in the science, but in the communication.

Throughout this process of reaching out to discover more about your prospects and customers, one essential element that needs attention is the way in which you talk to people. What tone does your text carry? What does the way you write say about your company? Does the text on your site and in your emails make you feel like a cold, distant corporation? Or is your language warm, giving expression to a more human, accessible side?

Whatever the data smarts you deploy, you'll find it hard to build any real sense of relationship if your copy doesn't match that intention.

Relationships Can't Be Built on Corporate-Speak.

Corporations have a reputation for being aloof and distant, uncaring and in pursuit only of profit. Putting aside those corporations that really are guilty as charged, other companies that would like to create a genuine relationship with their customers all too often find their efforts sabotaged by the stiff formality of the text they write. As an example, here is a passage of text taken from the "Corporate Citizenship" page of the Ford Motor Company Web site:

> At Ford Motor Company, we endeavor to become a leading contributor to a more sustainable world. Corporate citizenship is an integral part of every decision and action we take. Corporate citizenship focuses on who we are as a company, what we offer in the marketplace, and how we conduct our business. We aspire to be one of the most respected, admired, and trusted companies in the world.

While Ford's intentions may have been good, if the idea was to position the company as a fellow citizen on this planet, the company's use of language undermines its efforts. Real citizens don't talk that way. Real citizens don't have their words crafted by the people in the PR department. Nor do they say strange things like "Corporate citizenship focuses on who we are as a company." How can citizenship focus on something? If Ford was really interested in developing a relationship with its customers, it might have considered writing in a way that is more easily understood.

Without changing the basic message, here's how Ford might have better expressed itself:

> At Ford Motor Company we try hard to follow business practices that are sustainable in the long term. As a company we are aware of the impact we have on the planet around us. This awareness shapes who we are as a company and how we conduct our business. We are working hard to earn your trust.

Simpler language. Simpler concepts. Simpler promises. When you read this version you come much closer to a sense that this is a company that you can connect with as a human being. While the first version appears to deliberately create a distance between the company and its public, the second version reduces that distance and increases the sense that having a relationship with such a company is within the bounds of possibility.

Of course, this doesn't mean to say that the writer of the first version somehow failed in a gallant attempt to connect with his or her readers. In many instances companies will deliberately make the meaning of what they say both obscure and ambiguous. That prevents people from holding them to anything that might sound like a promise. It means they needn't be held responsible. When this happens, it's unfortunate for a number of good reasons. But one thing is for sure: Copy that distances the reader will undermine any ambitions you may have to build relationships with your customers online. It doesn't matter what software you deploy or how rich the offers are that you make; if the text doesn't ring true, you may well buy yourself some customers, but you certainly won't build yourself any relationships.

The Language of Permission.

When Seth Godin wrote his book, *Permission Marketing*, he was the first to effectively articulate the need for a different way of marketing within the online environment. In a shared space where the voices of the customers are as loud as those of the marketers, traditional marketing practices become harder and harder to justify. Not only do marketers have to compete within a very fragmented market, but that market is also hugely oversupplied. Hundreds of thousands of ecommerce sites are all competing for smaller and smaller slices of their customers' attention. When those online businesses start trying to raise their voices with traditional advertising methods, the message is drowned out. It simply ceases to work. The tried and trusted equation that told marketers that the more they spent on advertising, the more revenue and profits they would generate, doesn't work any more.

Seth Godin's book set out to describe a different path. First, before pitching your sale, solicit permission from your audience. While the basic idea of asking permission had been practiced by direct marketers for many years, it had never been applied to the Web. For the Web, permission marketing is a natural fit. It guides the way toward building relationships with customers based on permission and on trust. Customers and prospects alike become willing recipients of your marketing messages.

The concept of permission marketing became widely embraced almost immediately. It was a message that everyone wanted to hear. In fact, a recent search at Google for the term "permission marketing" delivered over 31,000 results. Unfortunately, while everyone talks the talk, very few marketers have really committed themselves to building relationships based on true permission. An atmosphere of "we have to meet this quarter's projections" works against permission marketing. But relationships can't be built within a time frame determined by your investors. It's a long-term process. It takes time to build relationships that have any real chance of survival.

Those who claim to practice permission marketing fall into two camps. There are those who are making genuine efforts to take that course because they see that traditional advertising approaches have a limited future online. And there are those who pay lip service to the notion of permission, but have no intention of turning that permission into a relationship based on trust.

Those who simply pay lip service to the idea of building relationships based on trust underestimate the degree to which people can accurately read between the lines of what companies say. While your customers may not be able to articulate what they feel, they will get a quick and accurate sense of how sincere you really are. Corporate-speak will score very poorly when it comes to communicating sincerity. Using a simpler, more human approach works better.

Here are two examples that show how the way in which you write can make all the difference in the world. Both of these emails were sent out without explicit permission, but both attempt to begin to generate the beginnings of a relationship.

First, here's an email from Amazon.com:

Dear Amazon Customer,

As someone who recently purchased from us for the first time (using this account), you've just begun to explore what we think

is the best shopping experience anywhere. Come see why—check
out these fun and convenient features.

Following this introductory paragraph, a number of links
directed the reader to some interesting features at the
Amazon site. Or more accurately, these are features that
Amazon feels are interesting. And that pretty much sums up
the tone and feeling of the message. The salutation "Dear
Amazon Customer" is about as dry as it could be, and the
content of the message says, more or less, "Hey, we noticed
you bought something, and we think you'll like our site
because it's terrific. We think it's fun and convenient too." In
other words, it's all about what Amazon thinks and has very
little to do with you.

By way of contrast, here's an email from The Motley
Fool at Fool.com. The purpose is the same, but the approach
and style are very different:

Dear Fool,

After taking a peek at our message boards today, we noticed that
you posted your first message on our site. Fantastic! First of all,
thank you very much for participating in our community—a community whose mission is Learning Together. Second, we'd like
to point you to some links that might be helpful.

First, the "Dear Fool" salutation sets the tone from
the outset. Stuffy corporations don't talk like that. Nor do
corporations say that they have taken a "peek" at their
message boards. But regular people do. Real people make
up comic salutations and use words like "peek" and when
they get excited they might even say, "Fantastic!" Immediately, the writers at Motley Fool have made their
site a lot more human and have taken a big step toward
making the reader feel at home. From there it's not such
a big step to start building a relationship. It's in the
language.

Sign-up pages and emails are just two of the places where the language of permission can make a real difference. Once you have found a style and voice that you feel will sincerely connect with your audience, you should begin to apply that approach across all of your online activities.

Make Your Language Match the Relationship.

As with any relationship, it's important online to match your tone and style to the level of relationship that has been achieved. If you've been doing business with a customer for the last three years online, you shouldn't be talking to that customer in the same tone you would use with a stranger. That's a missed opportunity. By the same token, if the relationship is new, you shouldn't sound like an old buddy.

Here's an example of some email text that gives the appearance of having come from someone who knows you quite well:

Dear Jack,

I can't believe Christmas is almost here. In New York we're expecting snow. . . a white Christmas. As I look back on the last year I realize how truly fortunate my family has been and I have become even more aware of those around us who are less fortunate.

The tone is very personal, but the email is actually part of a bulk email from the CEO of FreeLotto.com. However warm and fuzzy the CEO may be, this is not a credible tone to use when addressing thousands of lottery players. Even if the writer were absolutely sincere, the tone is too familiar for the circumstances. This kind of writing falls foul of some basic rules of email etiquette that were laid down by individuals a long time before commerce came to the Web. That is to say, don't presume to become too familiar when you're new to the conversation.

When you receive that first permission, write the follow-up text, whether at your site or through email, in a way that recognizes the moment for what it is—a beginning. If the relationship continues and survives over time, it's appropriate that your tone should change as well. Match the language to the moment.

Take the Fear Out of the Relationship.

Whenever any company tries to sell something to a customer, there's a degree of fear to be overcome. Here are some of the things your customer might be asking herself. Can I trust this company? What if I need some help in choosing the right product to buy—will the people who work there guide me in the right direction? Will the shipping and handling charges be reasonable? What if the product doesn't work? Is there a good guarantee, and can I really trust it?

When you're doing business online, there are some other legitimate fears that cloud a prospect's mind. Will this company still be around in six months? What happens with the personal information I give? What will the company do with it? And how about my credit card number? I've heard stories of hackers stealing credit card information off Web site servers. Will the product actually arrive, and what if I want to return it?

Overcoming fear is a key sales objective even in the offline world, but it's even more important online. The Internet is a relatively new place when it comes to spending money and making purchases. There are a lot more uncertainties online compared with those that people experience when driving out to the local mall. People in the business of marketing online very quickly forget what it's like to be new to the Web. An experienced user may feel very casual and comfortable about making purchases online, but that's not the norm. Millions of regular people would like to buy online but fear the experience. And who is to say that they are wrong?

There are a number of issues to be addressed when it comes to minimizing the customer's fear of making that purchase. First and foremost, companies have to address those fears seriously and take positive steps to reassure their online customers. Companies online have to sound trustworthy. Their voices have to calm the fears of their jittery prospects. And those voices have to be communicated through the way in which you write for your site.

Here is some text taken from one of the sign-up pages at Barnes & Noble.com:

> As a customer of Barnes & Noble.com you will occasionally receive notifications sent by Barnes & Noble.com about new services, features and special offers we believe would interest you. If you'd rather not receive these announcements and special offers, please uncheck this box.

The tone is very corporate and lifeless. It is also a touch strident, telling you what will happen when you sign up. Both the content of the message and the style in which it's written suggest a paternalistic approach that is very common in the offline world of marketing. While this tone may work well offline, it does nothing to reassure customers who may already feel nervous about making their first Barnes & Noble.com purchase. And if that first purchase never takes place, you have no relationship on which to build future revenues.

By way of contrast, here is a short passage from a sign-up area at HealthandAge.com:

> We will not send unsolicited emails or use any other form of communication to reach you unless you have explicitly given us permission to do so. Privacy is a real concern for HealthandAge.com—read our Privacy Statement here

The message is a great deal more reassuring. The first half of the second sentence, "Privacy is a real concern for HealthandAge.com" is refreshingly simple and clear. The writers could have said something like, "At HealthandAge.com we are committed to the provision of an online environment that strives to protect the privacy of our visitors." Twice the number of words and less than half the meaning. Very often, a simpler, more straightforward approach makes the message feel a great deal more human. They say it the way you or I would say it. They speak as individuals, not as a corporation. The voice of a corporation does nothing to reduce fear; it simply increases it. So the simpler and more human you can be, the better.

Of all the things that can poison relationships, fear sits high on the list.

Make It Easy to Start the Relationship.

Here's another aspect to the "fear" of doing business. Part of how you can make a customer feel more comfortable about trusting your company online is to take the adversarial edge out of the encounter as quickly as possible. At the beginning, if the customer is new to your company, the relationship has a default setting that is adversarial in nature. The customer wants to get the most from your company and pay as little as possible for it. Your company wants to get as much as possible from that customer on day one, because she has cost a lot of money to acquire, and the statistical chances of her becoming a long-term customer are pretty slim. As a result, you have a fight on your hands, albeit a small one. This adversarial element does little to help you create relationships that last. What makes the best sense is to do everything you can to start with a more trusting relationship from the first moment, while still attempting to close that first sale.

One site that addressed this problem head-on is 1-800-Flowers.com. For a while its homepage carried a photograph of Jim McCann, the CEO, with the words:

> Hi, I'm Jim McCann. Welcome to 1-800-Flowers.com.

If you clicked on that message, you got the following:

> . I would like to personally welcome you to 1-800-FLOWERS.COM and thank you for shopping with us.
>
> Our online store offers our customers an easy way to shop, whether you're looking for a special gift or something new for your home. Our commitment to our customers is simple; we offer a 100% satisfaction guarantee, 24-hour customer service, and our seven day freshness guarantee on all our floral products.

By showing a photograph of his face and putting his name to this guarantee and promise, Jim McCann did a pretty good job of taking away any sense that, as a company, it was out to get you. By stepping forward as a human being instead of hiding behind the site of a corporation, McCann was making himself personally accountable in the consumer's eyes. He was making a personal promise. You'll be 100 percent satisfied. He defused that adversarial moment and diluted any sense of fear that first-time customers might feel.

Of course, when you step into the limelight and make yourself accountable in this way, you had better be sincere and you had better deliver, or overdeliver, on every promise you make. Because if you don't fulfill your promises, the sense of betrayal and the damage done will be that much greater. A customer might half expect to be misled by a company and won't take it personally. But if the promise comes from a person, any disappointment that follows will be that much greater.

That's the double-edged sword of doing business online. The more personal you are, the better the response you'll receive. But at the same time, you'll be held to a much higher moral and ethical standard. You can no longer shrug, fold your arms, and say, "Hey, I'm sorry, but that's business. Don't take it personally." On the Web, everything is personal.

The Power of "Being There."

For individuals, the Web is a wonderfully connected place, bubbling over with character and personality. Within emails, live chat, and discussion lists, the Web is alive and filled with the voices of real people. But when those individuals arrive at a company's site, that sense of life and personality seems to just disappear. All of a sudden, users are faced with a complicated and often confusing interface that is counter-intuitive to just about every instinct they have, as a person and as a shopper.

There is a way to make your visitors feel more comfortable about being at your site. That approach simply involves "being there." Jim McCann of 1-800-Flowers.com was there on his site. Dave Thomas is right there on the Wendy's homepage. And Jay Steinfeld makes a point of "being there" at his site, NoBrainerBlinds.com.

On the NoBrainerBlinds.com homepage there is a small speech bubble near the top of the page. Whenever there's good reason to, Jay updates the text in that bubble. He may be talking about a particular season, a holiday, or a sales event at the store. In any case, that message is updated on a regular basis, and his regular customers watch to see what's there. One year, in the run-up to Valentine's Day, he had a line up there that read, "Tell Her you love Her with some New Blinds." Shortly afterward, his sales started to fall. Within a couple of weeks, his sales had dropped by almost

20 percent. It took a while to find the culprit. The problem was that he failed to update that message after Valentine's Day had passed. The implicit message to his customers? Nobody's home! He had ceased to "be there" because the page had become static and out of date. But within 48 hours of changing that message to, "March on in to March Madness." his sales climbed back up to where they were before. In Jay's own words:

> Every once in a while I get lazy or distracted and forget to attend to the bubble text on the home page. Almost every time I change it, it gets a rise in sales. You wouldn't think it would be particularly impactful, but people want to know you're there, AND that you're thinking about them. . . read that "caring" about them. . . and not being ignored.

That's a compelling reason to have an element on your homepage that gives people a sense that there is life behind the page. It's much easier to build a relationship with a person than it is with a page of HTML code.

Good Writing Can't Save a Bad Relationship.

You can employ the greatest copywriter in the world, but if the experience people have at your site doesn't live up to your promises, you are doomed.

Great copywriting cannot be used as a bandage to obscure the way that you really are. The way in which you describe your company's privacy policies cannot make a bad policy good. Simply saying that you care doesn't mean that you do. This is worth talking about because writers are often asked to add gloss and fill in the gaps.

Asking copywriters to make a product or service sound as good as it can possibly be is fine. But trying to mislead customers by representing your company as being somehow better than it really is, is something quite different. While you might be able to isolate disappointed customers who have discovered your true colors in the offline world, that's not so simple to achieve in the very connected world online. Word gets out, and it travels fast.

If your company has policies and practices that are not quite as you'd like them to be, just be honest about what they are. An imperfect policy stated honestly will do more good for your business than the same policy described in a manner that makes it sound better than it really is.

For instance, let's say you write the following about the return policy at your site:

> If for any reason you're not absolutely satisfied with your purchase, you can return it for a full refund. That's my personal guarantee! John Smith, President

That makes you sound good, and the boss has put his name to it. But let's say that the real policy, as written down in that meeting a few months earlier, is this:

> Full refunds on the purchase price, including taxes. But no refund on original shipping cost and the customer has to pay for the return shipping through FedEx or UPS.

The president's message glossed over the full truth of it. Over a short period of time a number of customers will have experienced the full truth behind the policy. And your relationship with them will have been ruined. And they'll doubtless share their disappointment with friends and family. The friendly tone of the copy didn't save the day. It just underlined the sense of being deceived. John would have been much better off saying something like this:

> If for any reason you're not absolutely satisfied with your purchase, you can return it for a full refund. That's my personal guarantee! The only cost to you would be the original and return shipping. John Smith, President

Does this sound a little less attractive? Yes, and John might want to review his returns policy. But better to be completely honest than to believe that a friendly tone will make up for a less than honest approach.

Keep It Fresh—in Every Way.

When particular elements of content on your pages are expected to change, then it makes sense to change them on schedule. But there are also many other pages on your site and messages within your outbound emails that have probably been sitting, unchanged, since the day they were first written. It might be that first welcome email you send out when people register at your site. Perhaps it's the introduction to your privacy policy or shipping instructions. Or your products and service descriptions. Or that last screen you serve when someone completes a purchase.

On the face of it, there may be no compelling reason to change any of the text in these places. If circumstances haven't changed, the facts on many pages and emails can stay the same. But the trouble with allowing old text to gather dust is that it may fall out of sync with the text you do update on a regular basis. The hope is that, as your business develops and your site evolves in response to customer feedback, the overall tone of your voice will change also. But when the voice on your homepage and in your weekly newsletter changes, so too should the copy on that welcome email—and in every other place that you attempt to engage your customers. If your voice is out of sync across different customer interaction points, it will inevitably raise some warning flags in your customers' minds. When your voice changes from place to place, according to when you last updated the text, you will give an impression of not being there. Or worse, you'll confuse your readers into wondering just who you are anyway.

Making the decision to rework text across the site and throughout a large number of outbound emails is a tough call. It's a lot of work and requires an investment from both writers and the IT people. But if you just leave old text the way it's always been, you run the risk of developing a disconnect between your company and your customers. And your relationship with them will suffer as a result.

Words have a powerful influence over the relationships that you build online. Remember, your customers are interacting with others online through text in emails, discussion lists, and live chat on a regular basis. There is a growing sophistication among the public online. As a result, in your business, it's time to "be there" online. It's time to make sure that your voice is sincere and that it's current. It's time to make sure that the words you use build genuine, personal connections between your company and your customers.

CHAPTER SIX

CAN THE WEB BE A STORE?

The Web as a Sales Environment

If you're online to sell something, there is a point at which you will win or lose. At some point in the process the sale needs to be closed. You need to craft your page and text to maximize the conversion rate of browsers to buyers. The copy on the screen needs to make people reach for their wallets and buy your product or service with a smile.

This is the point at which many experts get tangled over how and where to make the sale online. A symptom of their confusion is the poor conversion rates found on so many sites today. On many sites, the pages designed to make the sale actually drive users to distraction rather than to their checkbooks. The copy on those pages either makes no effort at all to promote a sale or, worse still, appears downright apologetic about asking people to part with their money.

Here are two ways *not* to go about closing the sale on your site or through an email.

The first way *not* to make an online sale is to take the route set out by people who believe that selling online is a dirty habit to be avoided by decent, right-thinking people. Don't leave your text hanging limp and passive in the hope that your customers will fill in the gaps for you. It's not the job of your customers to close the sale. They're within the most confusing shopping environment known to man (the Web), and they won't thank you for leaving them without direction or purpose. There comes a point in the process at a site when customers really want to buy something. They really want to buy it either because that's how they felt even before they arrived at your site or because you've done a great job of presenting the right product in the right way at the right time. Either way, many a sale is lost at the last moment. You need to promote the sale right up to the moment when that "Confirm Purchase" button is clicked, and beyond.

The second way *not* to make a sale online is to apply everything you ever learned in the offline copywriting world and use it, unchanged, online. You can't rush in like a bull in a china store and expect that the way you write offline will do just as well online. It won't. (Well, sometimes it will. But more of that later.) So how can it be done? How can a balance be achieved? How can you use the Web to build sincere relationships with your customers *and* to drive sales, both at the same time?

The simple answer is that you separate the two processes. Don't make an outright sales pitch at a point when you're writing something designed to grow or cement a relationship. And don't try building the relationship at the moment when you're trying to close a sale.

The more interesting answer lies in the fact that building relationships and making sales pitches concurrently is nothing new and speaks to the fascinating complexity of the relationships between customers and the companies they buy from.

Building Relationships and Sales Together.

The Web provides a wonderful opportunity to build relationships with your customers, because it's such a uniquely interactive space. The Web also has great potential as a sales channel, because it is so responsive. But can you do both? Can you build a sincere, one-to-one relationship with customers and still present them with a hard sell and accept their money? Of course you can. Relationships that are both social and commercial in nature have been a part of our lives for centuries.

Walk down to your corner store, if you still have one, and say good morning to the owner. Maybe he's known you since you were a kid. He asks about your mom and then takes your money for the loaf of bread you're buying.

Or you're playing golf with an acquaintance who also happens to be your dentist. Can you enjoy your game on a purely social basis? Of course you can. He's not going to try selling you some dental work halfway through the eighteenth hole. But come your next appointment, he may say, "Great game we had. We must get out on the course again soon. OK, open wide now."

And there you can see that shift between the social and commercial aspects of the relationship. Does the dentist know that when he plays golf with you on a purely social basis, he is also cementing the professional relationship between the two of you at the same time? Absolutely. In that case, is he being insincere and devious when he plays that game of golf? Not if he's any kind of friend. And if he is being insincere, he'll quickly lose both your friendship and your business.

Or perhaps you're taking a client out for drinks and dinner. You have a great meal together and find that your kids are the same age and into the same, pounding music. It's a wonderful evening and enjoyed by all. The next morning, you slip on your business suits and sit across the table from each other to start some serious negotiations.

One of the beauties of the Web is that you can use it to create similarly complex and potentially rewarding relationships. You can use one-to-one emails and newsletters to connect with customers, offering advice, listening to feedback, and growing the relationships. The tone can be personal and social in nature. Then, on your Web site or with the next email, you can connect again with that same person, but this time you can be pitching to make a sale.

Of all sales environments, the Web is best suited to growing relationships that are both social and commercial in nature.

Understand the Members of Your Audience and Their Expectations.

When it comes time to pitch that sale, the first thing to understand is the nature of your audience. How do your prospective customers feel about the Web, and what are their expectations from your site? Not everyone online is the same. In fact, the hundreds of millions of people who are emailing, chatting, sharing, and shopping online represent the same diversity you'll find in the land of bricks and mortar. So there is no one rule, no single solution, when it comes to how one should write to close that sale.

Here are two examples of very different online communities, from both ends of the spectrum.

Slashdot.org describes itself as "News for Nerds, stuff that matters." The site was launched in September 1997 and is ground zero for smart nerds with strong opinions about software, privacy, Internet standards, and a host of other meaty topics. It's a community of participants, dominated by moderated posts from people with a great deal to say. High signal, low noise.

How would you write to this audience if you wanted to make and close a sale? With caution! If a participant were to promote her products or services within this forum, she would have to do so as one peer to another, not as a vendor to a prospect. The sales pitch would have to be presented in language that fits the culture of the site. Most such pitches would never survive the moderation process. Those that did would offer something of clear value to the readership and be presented in a style that was respectful of the space and context and not slick with persuasion.

At the other end of the spectrum is a site like AOL—although it's a stretch to describe such a vast range of properties simply as a site. (That said, AOL still has to work within the same monitor size as everyone else.)

One of the more controversial introductions on the AOL site was the pop-up. Pop-ups are those pesky windows that open up when you log on to AOL. Today, the AOL pop-up may be selling you some software to help tidy up your hard drive; tomorrow it might be pitching you a terrific printer at a deeply discounted price. These pop-ups are extremely intrusive and demand action, one way or another. Even if you don't want to check out the offer, at the very least you have to close the window. This kind of in-your-face promotion is typical of the offline world, but is usually considered a horrible breach of netiquette.

The language in these pop-ups also sounds like it was lifted directly off the pages of that piece of unsolicited junk mail that arrived at your home this morning. Here's one example:

> John Smith, as an AOL member you are entitled to
> **Try any of these great magazines FREE!**

Here's another:

> **STOP TRYING, start talking!**
> AOL selects the Best!

Use your voice to type with AOL's Point and Speak! It works great with AOL e-mail, instant messaging and more! Get a 30 day risk-free trial!

So what's happening here? Has AOL lost its collective mind? Has it forgotten that the online space is not just a virtual showcase for its latest junk mail? Well, AOL has long confounded its critics by understanding the online experience a lot better than many self-proclaimed Internet pundits.

Here's how AOL came to write that way and throw up those horrible pop-ups, and why they work. AOL attracts regular people who are new to the online experience. These people don't know what "http" stands for, nor have they heard of Usenet. They don't know what netiquette is or have aspirations to number themselves among those people who "get it" online. These are ordinary people who have heard about the Internet and want to check it out. Do they realize that AOL is not the Internet? Often they don't, and they probably wouldn't care either. What they do care about is a simple experience and a place where they can find what they want—without getting lost among hundreds of thousands of confusing sites on the "real" Internet.

How does all this make a difference? The expectations of AOL's audience are very different from those who have been "online" on the "real" Internet for a while. AOL users don't belong to a culture that frowns on selling online. They have no history of that culture or access to it. It comes as no surprise to them to be "sold to" online. Yes, many will find the pop-ups irritating and close the window in a hurry, in the same way as they'll toss out that morning's junk mail. But the math still works. Enough people make a purchase to make it worthwhile. Would writing those pop-ups in a much softer, less overt way increase sales? No, it wouldn't. If AOL knows one thing, it's how to test pop-ups. Good old-fashioned sales copy does the trick just fine.

So how you write your sales text on your site will depend to a significant degree on where, on the scale of Slashdot to AOL, you believe your company fits in. How sophisticated are your users? For how long have they been online?

And wherever you put yourself on that scale, plan to nudge yourself a little bit further toward the AOL end of the spectrum. Because chances are you can sell a little harder than you think you can. With care, with honesty, with sincerity. But it's OK to make that sale!

Is there some contradiction here? How can one move on from an offline writing style and still end up using the same approach to sales copy? There is no contradiction. You can still use copy that is written with a view to making the sale, and you can still use phrases and words that have proved to be effective offline. Does the word "free" work as well online as it does in traditional advertising? Yes, it does. Free gift. Free shipping. Free gift-wrapping. Free upgrade. Free download. Free software. Free music.

It's not the sales element that you can't bring online; it's the way in which you do it. The key to making the pitch online is to make it at the right time, in the right place, and with the right tone.

Times When Customers Want to Be Sold To.

You're lining up for tickets for the baseball game. Your son wants the more expensive seats, but you say no and opt for the cheaper tickets, because that's what responsible parents do. Your son says, "Aw, come on—it's not much more!" Then the ticket guy behind the counter says, "Ten bucks more buys you a much better seat!" "No," you say, and buy the cheaper ones. As you take your seat you think, "Dammit, if that guy had pushed me a little harder, I'd have loved those better seats." Then you turn around and apologize to your son.

Or you're buying a camera. It's taken you months to choose the brand and model you want, and you finally find a store that carries it. What do you want the sales assistant to do? You want him to make that camera sound absolutely great. You want to hear that the store's service policy is second to none. You want to be sold—because you want that camera and you want to feel good about the purchase.

You read an ad for a PDA you've been thinking about buying and come away a little disappointed because you wanted the ad to sound better. You wanted to read a better selling job so that you'd feel good enough to go out and buy the product.

In short, it's simplistic to say that people never want to be sold to and resent every marketing and sales message that comes their way. It's just not so, even on the Web. For consumers who actually want to buy something, there are few things more frustrating than finding something they want, but not finding a sales message there to help them make the purchase decision.

The Web is knee-deep in millions of abandoned shopping carts that were being used by people who really wanted to buy something but didn't. Much of the time, the reason for abandoning those carts comes down to the poor usability level of the site. But another major cause of shopping cart abandonment is the failure of the site to make and complete the sale. The outcome? A disappointed prospect who will likely never analyze the reasons why he or she gave up but will nevertheless think twice before coming back to your site.

The sales process is part of the service you provide. It's part of what your customers are looking for and hoping for. Customers won't always resent the idea of being sold to. It's part of what they expect. It's part of the familiar web of relationships they have built up with the companies they buy from. They know the young man at the fast-food window will try to get them to buy those fries. They know that the computer salesperson will try to sell them extra peripherals and software. And that's OK. They can always say no. But if salespeople stopped selling, many customers would end up not buying those things that they really wanted. And they would feel disappointed.

The Downside of a New Sales Environment.

In the early days of the Web, those intrepid shoppers who embraced the Web as a place to buy things supplied their own sales momentum. These were the early adopters. They didn't need to be directed down simple sales paths through a site, nor did they need to read strong copy that would persuade them to make a purchase. The first people who came to shop online were a retailer's dream come true. They came with a mission and a passion. That mission was to be among the first to use the Web as a new place at which to shop. And even for those that followed the true leaders, there was a curiosity that drove them to figure out how to use this strange, complex shopping experience (the same curiosity that drove them to click banner ads with such frequency and naïveté in the early months and years).

The trouble is, everyone has moved on from the days of early adoption of shopping on the Web. It's old hat now. Millions of people are doing it. So shoppers no longer have the zeal of a new convert to drive them through page after page of sales-unfriendly screens. It's time for marketers online to become a little more realistic. It's time to recognize that your Web site is just another sales channel now. As with a direct-mail letter, you'll find that you lose prospective customers between screens and pages. You need to address that now by adding copy that advances the customer from one stage of the sale to the next. You can no longer expect your visitors to provide their own momentum and drive.

Figuring Out When and How to Pitch the Sale.

Marketers online have yet to find the exact right balance when it comes to pitching the sale online. How hard you sell, and how early on in the relationship, depends on who you are, what you're selling, and what the mindset is of your audience. If you're selling Viagra for $9.95, then you're going to open with both guns blazing. The members of your audience expect it, and they don't want a relationship with you anyway. But if you're selling financial services or medical services, as two examples, you're better off investing more time building up a trusting relationship before you let loose with the sales pitch.

Most companies fall somewhere in the middle ground. Yes, there is potential for a relationship of some kind. Or if not a relationship, then at least a sense of trust and respect. And of these companies, perhaps the majority still feel a little too shy about making, closing, and keeping the sale. It may be that people are still held back by that old netiquette sense of selling online being a bad thing. More likely, development groups and agencies just don't have the copywriting skills on hand. Or if they do, they are not using those writers in the right places or giving them sufficient authority to get the job done right.

In any event, it's time for marketers to recognize the need to sell a little harder online and help their customers complete their purchases. Persuading and helping your customers to find and buy what they want will make them feel good, and happy that they found your site. Making the sale is part of the service you provide. That's how selling becomes a key element in how you build successful relationships with your customers.

CHAPTER SEVEN

CLOSE THE SALE

When and How to Close the Sale Online

Millions of people spend hours and hours looking for a site that carries a certain product or service they want. When they find that site and visit it for the first time, those first few moments are crucial. Will they stay or will they leave?

Over the first two seconds at your site, a new visitor will receive a number of first impressions, each overlaying the others. Your visitors will get a quick sense of whether or not you have what they're looking for. Can they see it right there on your homepage? If not, do the images and text links on your homepage give the impression that what they want will be easy to find? At the same time, they'll get a feeling for what kind of company you are from the design and overall appearance of the page. Is this a classy place? Does it inspire confidence and trust? Finally, they'll also get a sense of your voice and style from the major headings and subheads that are found in and around the center of your homepage. Web users are likely to read that text before they look at any images, and the first place they look is in that center area.

If your site survives that first, cursory glance, visitors will decide whether to stay or hit the "back" button. Your task at this moment is to solicit some kind of action. Get them to sign up for something, to register, to make a purchase—or even to click through to another page on the site.

Start the Sale from Your Homepage.

One of the keys to maximizing the conversion rate of browsers to buyers on your site is to understand the points at which your visitors are most receptive to sales messages. These are the points at which visitors both expect and want you to encourage and enable a sale.

The first point at which someone may want to be sold is on your homepage, at the moment they first arrive. If they have arrived at your site through a search engine, for example, then their interest in what you sell is already foremost in their minds. They've been looking for something specific, entered that word or phrase into a search engine, and been delivered to your homepage. If they find what they're looking for, that moment is golden. So don't be shy; tell them how great that product really is.

While it makes sense to feature some key products or services on your homepage, you also need to cater to those people who don't see what they are looking for at first glance. In addition to being a shop window, your homepage also needs to draw visitors deeper into the site to find those products or services. You need some headings and links that actively draw users into the site. You need copy that enthusiastically solicits your visitors' attention and interest.

You can't feature your entire site on the homepage, so you need that page to be selling what you have at other levels within the site. Whether it's to sell a featured product or to persuade someone to click through to another page, your homepage has to drive that action, start that sale.

Where to Use a Copywriter.

Be sure that you're selling your wares effectively on the pages where you show and describe them. The Web is littered with descriptive text that is dry, dead, and without any redeeming qualities. In many cases that text was written by someone ill-prepared for the job. It's curious that companies should spend so much on their software and yet invest so little in making the sale to the customer. After all, with no sales, a business has no future, and the software it purchased becomes just another valueless asset with nowhere to go.

Here's how one site describes a high-end Panasonic cordless phone:

4 GHz/900 MHz Twin Band Transmission Design Shock-Resistant, Splash-Resistant Design2 Spread Spectrum Technology (SST) Our longest range SST technology to date All-Digital Answering System (15 min.) Call Waiting Caller ID Caller ID Pager Call 1 Digital Duplex Speakerphone Voice Prompts & Time/Day Stamp 2-Way Paging/Automatic Intercom Dual Antenna System Backlit 3-Line LCD Display on Handset 50-Station Caller ID Memory & Dialer 1 30-Station Phone Directory & Dialer Navigator Key Headset Jack & Belt Clip Call Screening, Skip/FF, Repeat/Rewind, All/Individual Erase Fast 7-Hour Battery Charging System Up to 8-Hour Talk Time4 Color: Titanium-Silver (also available in Metallic Black)

That was it, the full product description. It leaves a little to be desired, doesn't it? They might have done better with the following:

This Panasonic phone gives you the freedom you always wanted with your home office. Now you really can walk free, inside and out, in the knowledge that you'll never miss an important call. And if more important things—like blowing out those birthday candles—mean you can't pick up, you can relax in the knowledge that your Panasonic cordless comes with a digital answering system. For full technical details, <u>click here.</u>

This second version is not exactly hard sell. There's nothing pushy about it. But it does engage the reader's own imagination. It is inclusive. It paints a picture and offers an attractive version of the future that this product might support in some small way. And it's personal, one-on-one. If there is some technical information that needs to be included, go ahead, but link to it on a different page, or lower down on the same page. Not all visitors will want to read the technical details, so they shouldn't come first.

Here's another example, taken from a leading online jewelry store:

> Classic, elegant, and very necessary in every jewelry wardrobe is this diamond pendant. The mounting consists of four prongs with an 18 inch platinum cable chain. The diamond color is G/H with VS clarity. 1/4 carat total diamond weight.

How can a pendant be "elegant, and very necessary"? Toothpaste is necessary. Clean underwear is necessary. But not diamond pendants. That opening might have worked a lot harder, and touched its readers on a more personal level, if it had read something like this:

> Imagine the moment when you wear this stunning pendant for the very first time. Its weight, the flash of light from its diamonds, the way it rises and falls with every breath you take.

All of a sudden, you're finding a place in your readers' emotions and giving them one more, very powerful reason to make that purchase. You can go through the same process with any product or service, whether you're selling to consumers or to other businesses. There's always a way to write a description that gets a little closer to the reader on a personal level.

Say Enough to Close the Sale!

When it comes to selling physical products on the Web, copywriters are constantly under pressure to reduce the length of the copy they write. Experts tell them that people don't like to read online. Well, there's another side to that argument. Put simply, if you don't give your prospects enough information, they simply won't make the purchase.

The Web is not a great place from which to sell a product. People can't touch the item in the same way that they can in a store. They can't pick it up or try it out. All they have in front of them is one or two low-resolution photographs and that snippet of often sterile description. Usually, when products are being described on a site, the prospect first sees a short description next to a thumbnail photo. That piece of text is necessarily short, because it's usually on a page where there are several other thumbnails and short descriptions. But once you click on that thumbnail and are taken to a page that shows just that one product, that's where the longer text is. And this is the point at which that long text is usually still too short.

You've invested a great deal of money in getting your prospects to that page, so why lose them by not saying enough about the product? Why leave them with unanswered questions about some of the details you left off? Maybe you think that the people who need to know more will use your live-help service or maybe pick up the phone and call you. Some will, but most won't.

If you go to the Web and try, for instance, to buy a VTech 900-MHz cordless phone, you'll find plenty of vendors. Out of a random selection of three, one site used 31 words to sell the phone, another used 64, and the last, iQVC, used 628 words. Chances are that iQVC sells a lot more phones than the other stores.

Here's how iQVC uses its first 99 words:

Superior voice clarity. . . Extended range. . . Convenient features. For one week only E103586– VTech 900MHz Phone/Answering System with Caller ID and Headset, (QVC Price ~~$119.82~~) is just $99.82, only $69.82 after an iQVC Exclusive $30.00 Mail-In Rebate from VTech.

Save up to $50.00 for a Limited Time The Special Price and Mail-In Rebate from VTech are available for a *limited time only*. After Monday, April 16, 2001 at 9 a.m., ET, this low, low price goes back up to the regular price of $119.82. And, the Mail-In Rebate expires Thursday, May 31, 2001 at 11:59 p.m. ET. Order yours today and save!

The company is not wasting any of the early lines of text on technical specifications. Rather, it's going straight for the text that it knows will make the sale. For consumer electronics online, a great price matters.

If you're going to use a long description, it's important that you get the sequence right. You have to feed the information in a way that none of the vital facts are too far down the list. You don't want everyone to read every word. In fact, you're hoping to get most people to make the decision to buy after the first couple of paragraphs. The text toward the end gets more and more technical and incidental. It's there to pick up the stragglers, the people who really want to know everything before they commit to the purchase.

This carefully constructed, longer copy is going to convince a lot of those people who bailed out of the other sites that offered only 30 or so words of description. In the right place and for the right product and service types, long copy is what you need to make and close the sale.

How long should the copy be for your particular business online? That depends a great deal on the value and complexity of the products and services you are selling. It takes a lot more copy to sell a camera than it does to sell a roll of film. All you can do is test. And don't be afraid of trying longer copy and tracking the conversion rates.

Make the Sale and Build Trust.

Can you make a hard sell early on in your encounter with new visitors and still earn their trust at the same time? Yes, you can. It ties in to the notion that at a certain stage customers want and expect you to try to sell them your product or service. It's why they came to the site in the first place. It's simply a matter of getting the sequence right.

To be able to close the sale, you first have to open with plenty of signposts that establish your credibility and sincerity. If your customer has received emails or newsletters from you prior to coming to the site to make that purchase, much of that credibility will have been established through your tone of voice and the manner in which you requested permission to keep in touch. If the customer is coming directly to your site, then up-front reassurances on the homepage can go a long way toward making new visitors feel comfortable. Remember, if your site isn't a household name, visitors will form a first impression based on what they see first. So be sure to get the relationship off on the right foot at your homepage.

As an example, the main block of copy on the homepage at Poolfence.com has been growing in length from its beginnings as a short, introductory block. It is now considerably longer and very conversational in its tone:

Good afternoon!

Life Saver has been providing baby, child, and pet safety solutions for residential swimming pools and in homes for over a decade. <u>Removable residential swimming pool fence</u> has proven to be an effective drowning prevention aid for more than thirty-five years in the United States, and due to its commitment to saving lives, dedicated Life Saver Pool Fence Dealers can now be found from coast to coast in many larger cities.

Toddler driving you nuts at home? <u>Then this is the place for you!</u> Practical child proofing tips that work in the real world for real families. Safety is kind of a boring subject, so we have written this do-it-yourselfer in-home guide for those that have a sense of humor. If you don't have a sense of humor, then you better get one fast if you're planning on raising normal children.

On the other hand, our attitude on <u>swimming pool safety</u> is rather hardcore. Accidents are unforeseeable events which cannot normally be avoided. A toddler falling into an unprotected home pool and drowning or becoming a near drowning victim is not an "accident."

The **Discussion Center** is back! Post any questions or thoughts you may have and get real parent answers.

We'd like to use this space to thank as well as inform. We at Life Saver really appreciate you visiting our site and taking the time to learn about child safety and pool safety.

Like you, we're parents, and your love of your children is why we exist. So, when you're reading our <u>child safety guide</u> or about <u>removable mesh pool fence</u>, think about how you can apply the things you learn to your life. We've learned so much writing this site for you and we learn more as we add and enhance it every day. We can always learn more. If you have a suggestion or idea, <u>tell us</u>.

Thank you for reading and enjoy the site. Don't forget to save us as a favorite place. We're always changing.

There are experts by the barrelful who will tell you that this copy is far too long and won't be read by anyone. Not true, says Eric Lupton, the man behind the site and this very profitable business. Here's his reasoning behind the length and style of text that he uses:

We started out with brief, precise copy on the home page and have slowly lengthened it. The longer it gets, the more people seem to connect with the site. Our product is one geared toward parents protecting their children, so you need to take that extra space to really let them know they can trust you. The more inviting and personable, the better. They have to know you are real.

"They have to know you are real." That's a pretty good catchphrase to keep in mind as you write your next email message or Web page. Let the people you connect with know you are real. When you do that, you have the beginning of a relationship based on trust.

Once you have established trust, once your visitors feel comfortable about taking the plunge and doing business with you, then you can start leading them up to the moment of making the sale.

Understand How Testimonials Work Online.

The use of customer testimonials goes back to the time of the caveman. Here's the core of the process: "Hey, if you don't believe me, ask Harry, a satisfied customer." Testimonials are used to add credibility to your sales pitch. And they work extraordinarily well.

Testimonials work on TV, in print, and in direct mail. "I lost 20 pounds with XYZ and have never looked or felt better!" When your customers speak out on your behalf, they're speaking one-to-one with your prospects. The prospects feel reassured that they are receiving the views not just of the company, but also of other individuals just like them. The assumption is that these testimonials are completely unsolicited. In reality, this isn't always the case. Many an "unsolicited" testimonial has been edited and sometimes rewritten so that it sounds better and covers the right ground. But that aside, customers like to hear from other customers about their experiences with a particular company or product.

The same is true online. Not many Web sites use testimonials, but they could. It makes sense to add the experiences of other customers to your site. In fact, it makes more sense to do this online because of the very attributes that make the Internet unique as a business environment. Online, your customers are better connected with one another than ever before. They are used to checking out each other's viewpoints. They like to listen to one another.

In fact, the Web extends and radically shifts the whole concept of traditional customer testimonials. Online buyers don't have to depend on sound bites from happy customers being shown on your site. They can go to outside sites like Planetfeedback.com and Epinions.com. These sites publish the third-party opinions of tens of thousands of customers. They rate products, services, and the sites from which they are available, complete with unedited comments from both happy and unhappy customers.

Some sites, like Dell.com and Shell.com, deliberately host the full range of customer opinions within community areas on their own sites. They benefit directly from the positive comments and gain respect for posting the negative comments. But this kind of open community isn't right for everyone, or for every site.

However, if you want to add traditional testimonials to your pages, be aware that this isn't TV or a direct-mail brochure. Because of the more open communications that customers are becoming accustomed to online, because of sites like Epinions.com and other feedback aggregators, the language of the pitch has to change a little. Your testimonials need to be toned down by a few degrees. Don't rewrite a customer's natural voice to sound more excited or breathless. Use the verbatim words of your customers.

Also, using the same testimonials in your print brochures, month after month, may work well for your business. But if you leave the same comments on your site for too long, you're missing an opportunity. The Web is a place where everything moves, everything changes. Do the same with your customer comments. Collect new ones; keep them fresh; update them. This way you're adding new content to your pages and giving a strong impression to repeat visitors that a lot of happy people buy from your site. When you regularly update those testimonial messages, it shows that you're in touch with what your customers are saying and you're eager to share their views with others. Although not as open or interactive as a community area, the strong use of new and changing testimonials creates a very strong and supportive context for your sales messages.

A side benefit to showing a lot of fresh testimonials on a regular basis is that you'll suddenly find yourself forced to encourage your customers to tell you what they think. When this happens, you'll get into the habit of listening harder—to the good, the bad, and the ugly. Ultimately, you will build a better business by listening to everything your customers say. Post the great comments to your site and use the negative comments to improve the aspects of your business that customers find disappointing.

Keep Selling after the Purchase Is Confirmed.

Once a customer has clicked on that "Confirm Purchase" button, there is a temptation to consider that the sale is made and that your job is done. But that's not the case. First, if your site is set up for it, customers can cancel their orders before the orders have even been shipped. Second, buyer's remorse can cost you money through your customer service people if purchasers then call up or email you with concerns or inquiries about their orders. Worse, if they're not completely happy, they can return their order after it has been received.

Making the sale may give you a brief pause, a moment to catch your breath. But the sale has not ended. Confirmation pages on your site and follow-up emails should all be written in a way that is reassuring and makes customers feel good about what they've just bought.

Here's an example of the kind of bare-bones email that is typically sent out immediately after a purchase has been made:

Dear John Smith,

Thank you for shopping at futureshop.ca!

To check your current order status online, please visit https://www.futureshop.ca/orders/orders.asp. You may be required to login with your user name and password.

Here is the status of the following item(s) of your order (1612038) received on 18 Mar 2001, 10:10:02

Yes, it's great that the buyer gets confirmation of the purchase. But how about a little extra life? A little soul? Show some respect for the fact that someone has just typed in his credit card number and is now crossing his fingers and hoping that whatever he bought will actually turn up one day.

How about something more along the lines of:

Dear John Smith,

Congratulations on your purchase of the Canon PowerShot S10 Digital camera. Great choice! That's a big seller for us, so we know people like it a lot.

To check your current order status online, etc. . .

A little extra work for the IT staff with those variables? Sure it is. And you'll need some text variations to cover different products of different popularity. But if you look at the cost of postpurchase customer service and returns, isn't it worth making a little extra effort to help people feel comfortable with their purchase?

Here's an example from CircuitCity.com. This email wasn't sent out in immediate response to a purchase, but it was sent to CircuitCity.com customers:

> Dear CircuitCity.com customer,
>
> The nights are getting cooler, the days are getting shorter, and the leaves are getting ready to put on their spectacular annual show. It must be the end of the summer, and that makes us think of electronics. Of course, pretty much everything makes us think of electronics. We're CircuitCity.com.
>
> Starting Sunday, September 2, we'll have some offers you're not going to want to miss. Take a look!

It's a promotional email, but it creates a sense of familiarity with the reader through its use of humor. A shared joke like this works well with current customers. It makes readers feel that they are part of something—that they are sharing a joke with friends. While the purpose of this email is to promote a new sale to a current customer, it also works on another level, cementing the relationship with that customer even if he or she doesn't make another purchase right away.

Support the Sales Process at Every Point.

Making a sale through your site is not an isolated event without a past or future. Customers will make a purchase as a result of their complete experience with you prior to that moment of clicking the "Confirm Purchase" button. They may have been reading your newsletter or emails and may have been to your site three or four times prior to that day when they made their first purchase. It was the culmination of all the impressions they received that resulted in that sale. Will they come back and buy again? That will depend on the experience they have after making that first purchase. Was the shipping timely? Did their purchase delight them? Was your customer service impressive?

The copy at key moments on your site has to be written in such a way as to close the sale. But beyond that hard-hitting copy, the rest of your site and outbound marketing communications have to be written with a view to supporting that moment when the sale is closed. You can't make the sale in isolation. You can't have a site and a newsletter that is entirely passive and then expect one screen of hard-hitting text to make the sale on its own. The entire customer experience has to be created with a view to supporting the sale.

CHAPTER EIGHT

THINK LIKE A DIRECT MARKETER

Go for a Direct Response in the Spots Where It Really Counts

No, the Internet is not a direct-marketing medium. But yes, the Internet is a wonderful environment in which to practice direct marketing and to use direct-marketing techniques. Through the simple genius of hyperlinks, the Web is hugely responsive. And if you are selling from the Web, you depend absolutely on the responsiveness of the online space. If nobody clicks those links, you get no response, no sales, and in time, you're left with no business.

Over the years direct marketers have received plenty of bad press for not being quite as classy as regular advertising professionals. You'll find this in evidence in advertising agencies the world over, where the general advertising people who create the high-end TV ads, billboard campaigns, and glossy magazine awareness ads all look down on the direct-marketing teams. There is often a sense that direct marketers are the guys who weren't quite good enough to make the grade in the general agency. However, as much as the direct marketers are looked down upon, every agency has simply to follow the money in order to see what its clients really want. The last two decades have seen a persistent migration of cash away from awareness advertising and into the more accountable practice of direct marketing.

In the same way that the general agency people may look down on the direct marketers in the world of bricks and mortar, a similar dance is being played out in the world of marketing online.

With the origins of writing online lying in the hands of millions of individuals who cherish their pitch-free space, there is a sense of near outrage at the bold and brassy language of direct marketers online. How dare they bring their vulgar promotions, capitalized letters, and crass "Free" offers to the Web? It's understandable that people might mourn the passing of a commerce-free Internet, but in those areas online where business depends on sales, it will be the skills of the direct marketers that bring victory to those sites that care to listen. The Web is simply a direct marketer's dream come true.

The technology of the Web enables tight targeting to qualified groups of prospects. Hyperlinks allow for instantaneous responses. Backend software allows for immediate analysis of results and the ability to fine-tune the next day's offers. Testing can take place within hours, instead of weeks or months. The Web takes the key drivers of direct response and pumps them full of adrenaline. There is no hiding the fact that the Web gives direct marketers everything they want in a medium. And their presence online right now represents just the tip of the iceberg. So if you don't like the kind of future this may portray, it's time to hide. But if you like the idea of selling more, improving conversion rates, and building closer relationships with your customers, the direct-marketing expert is your best friend.

In addition, you don't need to be selling direct from your site to benefit from the knowledge of direct-response professionals. Wherever you want a visitor to take an action on your site, that is an instance of direct response. That action may be to subscribe to a newsletter, sign up for special offers, build a membership profile, or send an article or postcard to a friend. Whatever the action, more people will take it if you learn a few things from direct-response writers and designers.

Direct-Marketing Copywriters Know How to Drive Customers to Take Actions.

If you look over the shoulders of regular people trying to buy something online, here's a phrase you'll hear quite frequently:

So what do I do now?

Every time visitors to your site ask that question while trying to make a purchase at your site, you have failed. You've failed to give them the direction they need in order to complete their purchase. You and your development team may feel that it's obvious what your visitors should be doing next. But if first-time visitors can't figure it out, everyone loses. And the truth is that people need and want clear direction. They want it in a store, they want it in a catalog, and they definitely want clear direction online.

Take this morning's junk mail out of the trash and look at what direct marketers do when it comes to directing people from one point in the process to the next. If there was a letter in the package, somewhere in that text, probably toward the end, it might say something along the lines of:

Find out how to save $10 off Brand X! Read the enclosed brochure and complete and return the application form today. But hurry—this offer ends on April 25th!

On the brochure it might say:

You can make your $10 saving today with just three easy steps. 1) Complete the enclosed application form, 2) Enclose it in the pre-paid envelope provided, and 3) Mail it to us today!

On the application form itself it might say:

YES, please send me my Brand X today! I understand that if I reply before April 25, I'll save $10!

On the reverse of the pre-paid envelope it may say:

Have you completed and enclosed your application form? And don't forget—to receive your $10 saving, you MUST mail this to us by April 25th.

With a sales medium as simple and as familiar as direct mail, are all those directions necessary? Are customers really so dumb that they need repeated, repeated directions, all saying the same thing?

First off, customers aren't dumb. But if you think that your direct-mail piece or your Web site is engaging your visitors' entire, undivided attention, then perhaps you're the dumb one. For the writers and designers of direct-mail packages it would be a wonderful thing if people read everything is this sequence:

1. The envelope

2. The letter

3. The brochure

4. The application form

And it would be even more wonderful if they read each element from top to bottom, without missing a word. And it would be great if they weren't eating breakfast, watching TV, listening to the kids, and worrying about being late for work, all at the same time.

But what really happens is that the direct-mail package receives only a small slice of attention, and its contents are read in an infinite variety of sequences. That's why writers add directions in multiple locations and repeat key messages, time and time again. That's why no part of the package ever leaves the reader with any doubt about what he or she should do next.

Now try working your way through your own site, whether you're selling items, services, or simply registrations. How clear are the directions from one part of the process to the next? How often do you repeat key benefits? (Or did you think that mentioning that 10 percent discount once on the homepage was enough?) How large is the type that says "Checkout"? Is it hugely, blindingly obvious and clear? And anyway, why wouldn't you say:

CHECKOUT—with FREE gift-wrapping!

Repeat instructions on every page of the process. Keep them short and keep them clear. And if you have some key offers in place, like free shipping, product discounts, or whatever else—repeat those too.

Direct marketers know how to work with an audience that is giving them only a small slice of attention. In a heartbeat customers will apply their full attention to something much more interesting. It doesn't take much for someone to toss a piece of direct mail. And it takes even less for someone to click on that back button.

The Immediacy of *Now.*

According to eMarketer, a leading provider of Internet statistics, Americans go back to an average of just 13 sites on anything like a regular basis. Given that there are now millions of Web sites out there, 13 is a very, very small number. And only a few of those will be soliciting direct sales.

With that in mind, you need to be aware of how fragile your hold is on visitors to your site, and how unlikely it is that they will ever return if they don't register, sign up for your newsletter, or make a purchase on that first visit.

That first visit is also the time at which no relationship exists between you and your visitors, and they have no tie to your site. In short, your window of opportunity is very narrow indeed. You have just a few moments in which to engage their attention and hold it long enough for them to take at least one action at your site. That's why you need to persuade people to take some kind of action *now*.

You've seen from some of the examples above how direct marketers drive for immediate responses:

To receive your $10 saving, you MUST mail this to us by April 25th.

Direct-mail writers use the "by this date" device frequently. Ads on TV offer attractive incentives if viewers call the 1-800 number within the next 10 minutes. Radio stations entice listeners if they are caller number x, right after the sponsor message. The reason for driving immediate action is that once you lose your visitor's attention, you'll likely never get it back. It's now or never.

Taking the longer view, it makes sense to try to build a longer-term relationship with your online customers, based on trust and great service. To get to that point, you first need to solicit some kind of action from the first-time visitor, right now.

Here's an example of how, on its own site, eMarketer drives the moment on one of its sales pages. The page is designed to sell site visitors a one-year subscription to the eStat Database.

Here's the text on the two key buttons on the page:

Get a Free 24-hour Trial

and:

See it NOW. Take our Quick Tour.

And here's the sales text that accompanies those buttons:

INTRODUCTORY PRICE: The eStat Database is normally $2,500 per user for an annual license, but, for a limited time you can sign-up for a single-user annual license for only $1,250. Call 1.877.378.2871 for multi-user discounts or for more information. Buy Now

The writer of this page was very well aware of how easy it is to lose a visitor. Even for those people who are not ready to put cash on the table right now, there is the opportunity to try the service free for 24 hours or even take a quick tour. And when it comes to the pricing itself, you'll recognize key terms and devices that are commonly used in direct response advertising: "INTRODUCTORY PRICE" "for a limited time" "only $1,250" "Call 1.877" "Buy Now." Every aspect of this page, from its design to the words used, drives toward soliciting some kind of immediate action. Does this kind of "buy-now," direct-marketing approach cheapen the offer and the site? Not at all. The eMarketer site is a highly respected business-to-business site, and its brand isn't diminished at all by the use of copy that is designed to make an immediate sale.

The same approach can also be used through emails. Here's the introductory text from an email from Chapters.ca, a Canadian online bookstore that also has retail locations across the country:

REMINDER:

CHAPTER 1 MEMBERS SAVE 20% ON ALL REGULARLY PRICED BOOKS!

TONIGHT ONLY!

6:00pm UNTIL MIDNIGHT.

The purpose here is a little different. The company is using email to drive traffic to a physical store. But the focus on immediacy remains the same.

iQVC.com emails a daily special to everyone who requests it. This email goes out seven days a week, in HTML, and works hard to sell the single, featured product. There's no point in looking at yesterday's special, because these offers expire by the end of the day on which they are sent. After each product description, the reader is reminded of the need for immediate action with this text:

> This EXCEPTIONALLY LOW PRICE is good for TODAY, Monday— April 30, 2001 (Eastern time), ONLY. QVC's BEST VALUE for the day is Today's Special Value.

In other words, buy now or lose the special price.

Direct marketers know that asking for an action immediately drives more response than an open-ended offer. For those sites online that depend on customer action, it makes sense to learn from these lessons. And it's hard to imagine a commerce site that does not depend on customer actions at some point. Here are a few of the actions you might want visitors to take at your site.

- Register their name and email address.
- Sign up for a newsletter.
- Give you permission to send promotional emails.
- Download a program or document.
- Respond to an email.
- Interact with a customer service agent.
- Click on the "Confirm Purchase" button.
- Dial a phone number.

You can probably find another half dozen or so specific actions at your site. These are the actions that are key to building both immediate and lasting conversion rates for your business. So take a look at the copy that you use at these points. Does it drive immediate action? Do you press for a response right now?

In an environment that is as fragmented and as distracting as the Web, the success of your business will depend on how well you drive your visitors to take immediate action.

Recognize "Seducible Moments."

Jared Spool is the founder of User Interface Engineering and he likes to talk about "seducible moments." These are those moments when visitors to your site are at their most seducible. They have taken an action that indicates their interest in registering at your site, signing up for a newsletter, or making a purchase. Add to that list all those other customer actions mentioned in the section above. These seducible moments are golden because your visitors, by clicking through to a particular page, have indicated that they have a particular and immediate interest in taking that action.

So, once again, does your copy at those points recognize the user's state of mind? Does it speak to that brief moment of particular interest? Does it solicit immediate action or perhaps take the route employed by eMarketer, with the promise of a tour or a free trial?

All too often, copy is written for Web pages on the apparent assumption that each page receives the same amount, and the same quality, of attention. That's unfortunate, because the kind of attention received will vary considerably between different pages. At seducible moments, that attention is about as focused as you'll ever find it. And you need to take full advantage of that fact. That isn't to say that you should take advantage in any kind of manipulative way, but you should be helping your visitors complete actions at the moment when they are showing the most interest in doing so.

Don't be shy. When a customer wants to be seduced, go for it.

How a Direct-Response Writer Reduces Attrition.

A difficulty presented by the very fragmented sales path within a Web site is that you have to keep advancing the sale, screen after screen after screen. Using a direct-mail letter as an example of how one advances the sale, every sentence and every paragraph has to be constructed in such a way as to move the reader forward. This is particularly true of paragraphs. The end of every paragraph provides the perfect opportunity to stop reading. That's why writers of direct-mail letters butcher the accepted practice of starting a new paragraph with a new idea. If you do that, it means that the end of each paragraph ends with a closing, so it's complete. When that happens, it's much easier for people to stop reading and drop the letter into the garbage.

The whole point of direct-response writing is to keep your prospects reading, word after word, passage after passage, until you achieve your purpose, whatever that may be.

In the world of direct mail, the danger of losing the reader mid-sale is at its highest at the end of a page. That is why, in a really good direct-mail letter, you'll see that a sentence is broken in two, between the bottom of one page and the top of the next. When you do that, there's a far greater likelihood that the reader will turn the page to finish reading that sentence on the other side or other sheet. Once the page is turned, a major danger point has passed. Experienced writers become crafty in the ways of advancing the sales argument.

The skill of advancing the sale within a Web site is equally important because there are far more places at which you are likely to lose your reader. Every time someone has to click through to a new page, you lose people. Every time someone has to scroll down another screen, you lose people. Every time you ask someone to click somewhere for more details, you lose people.

The skill of writing to minimize losses along the sales path has not been widely applied to the Web. Usability and information architecture experts will look for ways to reduce the number of clicks and keep the process simple, but are they asking for help from copywriters as they work? In most cases, no.

Reduce Losses from Your Homepage.

Not every visitor will arrive at your site through your homepage, but most will. And most of those visitors will never move on from there. They'll take a quick look around and leave. Some will leave because they figure out that you have nothing of interest for them. But many more will leave because you've done nothing to keep them. Nothing on the homepage has either held them there or actively moved them on to the next page. This is a usability issue, an information architecture issue, and a copywriting issue.

To take another example from the direct-marketing world, consider the lowly envelope. No, a homepage is not the equivalent of an envelope. But it's useful to look at how envelopes work, simply to learn a thing or two about advancing a reader's attention. Envelopes and the few words on them are all that stand between a piece of direct mail and the recipient's trash can. One way or another, the text on that envelope has to arrest and reverse one's natural inclination to toss every piece of "sales-mail" that darkens your mailbox.

The purpose of the envelope is not to make the sale or even to get past stage one of making the sale. Its purpose is simply to persuade the recipient to take a look inside. That's all. Here are some examples of copy lines from envelopes:

Send for your FREE sample today!

Just look at what you've been missing!

Win a vacation for 4 in Florida

Your invitation is inside.

You just lost your cellular phone and . . .

All these examples have one thing in common. They drive the reader forward. They let you know that the good stuff is yet to come. They tell you that if you stop reading now, you'll be missing out.

It might be that none of these lines comes anywhere close to what you want to say on your homepage. But if the meat and the action and the rewards of your site are one or two levels down from the homepage, shouldn't you be doing something to drive people forward?

Look at the copy on your homepage now. It's likely made up of passive links and few headings here and there. How many of those links or headings are written in the active voice? That is to say, how many incite action or response? Or are they all passive?

Here are some examples of passive links and headings:

This week's specials

Digital cameras

Music best-sellers

And here are some more active equivalents:

Check out this week's specials . . .

NEW digital cameras inside . . .

Here's the music everyone is buying . . .

Yes, they are longer, and yes, that may well mean some changes are necessary to the page design. But try it out—take some of those passive snippets of text and add a little voice, a little action, and a little persuasion to them. Test the short and passive against the longer and active equivalents and see what happens. If the longer ones win, make some changes.

It is said by some usability and customer-experience experts that users come to the Web in a very goal-oriented frame of mind. They arrive at sites with a mission and want to achieve that mission with a minimum of fuss. That may be so, but it doesn't mean that your homepage has to sit there as a passive participant. It's OK to do whatever you can to engage each visitor's attention and drive that visitor forward into the site.

Learn About the Two-Stage Sell—and How to Apply It to the Most Fragmented Sales Environment of All Time.

If you come from a direct-marketing background or are in sales, you'll know about the two-stage sell. If you're not, here's what it is and how it works.

You're reading a magazine and a reply-paid card falls into your lap. You pick it up and read it: It offers a free guide to home insurance with some delectable offer thrown in to encourage you to fill in your name and address and mail the card. A week after mailing the card, you receive a glossy brochure complete with an application form. You read the brochure, like what you see, and then send in the application and a check. That's a two-stage sell. The card that fell out of the magazine had a single purpose, and that purpose was not to sell you insurance. The card's purpose was simply to get you to fill it out and mail it. It was designed to sell you the next stage, the brochure, not the final product.

The online environment is filled with multistage sells. At its simplest and easiest, an outbound email may be sent out to encourage people to visit your site or to look at a particular item or group of items on your site. As with the prepaid card, the purpose of the email is not to sell the products in question, but to get people to click through to the site. That's what the job of the email is. It's just the first stage.

As an example, here's an email that was sent out by WebMD:

> Breathe Free With WebMD Itchy skin reactions, runny noses, sneezing fits—and even severe asthma attacks. Whether you're reacting to pollen, dust, or the family pet, allergies can be really annoying. Although there's no easy cure, you can reduce their effects—and Breathe Free.
>
> WebMD's Breathe Free Allergy and Asthma special section features expert advice on how you can live a more allergy-free lifestyle, test your knowledge with allergy and asthma quizzes, and participate in a WebMD University online class instructed by William E. Berger, MD, author of Allergies and Asthma for Dummies. Check out the WebMD Breathe Free special section today http://breathe5.webmd.com.

Maybe they're just selling you on content here, but they still want to drive you to the page in question. The purpose of this email was to get you to click on that URL—http://breathe5.webmd.com. That's it; that's what this email was for. So one might ask why the URL was preceded by over 100 words of introductory text. Is it that tough a sell?

Do you really need more than 100 words if the sole purpose of the email is to move readers from their email to the WebMD site?

Something like this might have worked a little better:

> **Do you have asthma or allergies? Are breathing troubles taking the fun out of your life? Check out the WebMD Breathe Free special section. Click here. http://breathe5.webmd.com**

That would probably have done a better job because it got to the point a great deal faster. If you tell people too much in your introduction, whether it be in an email or on a web page, they may feel that they've read enough and don't need to click through to the next stage. Give them just enough to satisfy the needs of that stage alone. Move them on, keep them interested in what's coming next. Tell them enough, but not too much. In addition, people are receiving so many emails they are becoming less and less willing to read long blocks of text just to figure out what it is you want them to do.

Here's another example. It's an email that is apparently designed to drive the reader through to the company's site:

> **Spring is here . . .**
> **Save $5 Off Everything At iPrint!**
>
> Now is the perfect time to save BIG when you order your custom-designed products from iPrint! Everything from customized t-shirts and tote bags to personalized golf balls and business cards.
>
> Savings like this are a great way to start off your Spring!
>
> Design what you want today at iPrint! This limited-time offer expires on 04/03/2001!*
>
> **<u>Click Here to Order!</u>**

It starts off well with that $5 discount offer. Things like that work. People like to save money. But after that, it gets a little confusing. It says you can save big, but is that $5 all you get off if you order a whole box of customized t-shirts, tote bags, golf balls, and business cards? The offer is confusing. A $5 discount on a t-shirt sounds great, but as a discount on a box full of items, it sounds a lot less attractive. Ambiguity is a big turn-off for your customers. And then there's that link at the end, "Click Here to Order!" Well, the readers probably aren't ready to order. And if they click that link, will they end up having ordered something they don't want?

If your first stage is confusing and tries to extend beyond what it can reasonably accomplish, you'll run into trouble. Your readers will be confused and uncertain. And if they are uncertain, they probably won't even risk clicking on that link. At that point, this very simple first stage will have failed completely.

That last email might have done a little better like this:

Spring is here . . .
Save $5 Off Everything At iPrint!

That's $5 off your first order when you buy your custom-designed products from iPrint! Everything from customized t-shirts and tote bags to personalized golf balls and business cards.

This limited-time offer expires on 04/03/2001!

Click here to start saving!

Create Momentum along the Sales Path.

If you can engage readers and kick them into gear on your homepage, you then have to hold their attention through a number of additional pages in order to complete a sale. Once again, most sites take a very passive approach to this.

There is a belief, somehow, that the presence of a hyperlink is sufficient. Well, it's not. To drive and complete the sale, you need to take a much more active approach.

Here's an example from a popular gift site a few weeks before Easter. On the homepage, among other photos, it shows a candle in the shape of a bunny. The text that accompanies this photo reads:

Bunny candle $25

Click on the text or the image and you're taken to a page devoted just to showcasing the bunny candle. Here's the text:

Not every Easter Bunny delivers eggs and candy. This one casts a warm glow on a festive table set for family and friends. Simply lift the hand-molded beeswax bunny from the oval basket and light the candle inside. Naturally scented with sweet honey, the candle burns for about 10 hours, and when it's gone, just tuck a tea light inside to keep it burning brightly all season. Measures 4″ tall x 5″ wide.

A couple of inches beneath the description, as part of a really very small image, it says:

Add to bag

Click on the "Add to bag" link and, if you've completed a couple of fields correctly (easy not to), you're taken to a shopping cart page describing your selection. Perhaps the most prominent piece of text on this page—simply because it's in red and contrasts strongly with the black text surrounding it—reads as follows:

Total does not include tax and shipping, which will be calculated during checkout.

That's a three-screen process. The homepage, followed by a product page, followed by the shopping cart page. But there is nothing on any of these pages that has been written to deliberately drive the reader forward to the next screen. The homepage just shows the photo, the product name, and the price.

How about something like this:

Bunny candle $25—buy now for guaranteed delivery by Easter!

Again, there are a few more words there. But those extra seven words provide a reason to keep moving on, right now. Get their attention, and once you have it, try not to let it go.

The second page gives the full description, but does almost nothing to advance the sale. Nothing in the text suggests that the reader make that purchase right now. And the "Add to bag" button is quite separate visually, from the text anyway. The marketers, designers, and writers behind the site are simply waiting for their prospects to do all the work, to supply their own momentum. You can do that, but you'll get a much better conversion rate if you direct, guide, and encourage your prospects through the various pages that are necessary before the sale is confirmed. The sales path through a Web site is hugely fragmented. You need to nudge, to help move people along. Give them an incentive for moving along, screen by screen.

Even that "Add to bag" button could have been given a little more excitement by rewarding users for clicking the link:

Add to bag—and we'll add a free mystery gift.

A cheap sales trick? Not really. For as long as the device you employ helps your visitors achieve their goals, you're not manipulating them: You're rewarding them for taking a path they already want to follow. The reward is there not to manipulate, but to reduce attrition rates along the sales path. This approach works well, and people don't mind. When you look at the math, you'll find that every time you add some extra punch to your copy at a key point in the process, you'll be rewarded with a slightly higher conversion rate.

Try Another Direct-Marketing Classic.

Deep in landfills all over the western world are the remnants of buckslips—small dollar bill–sized slips of paper that go into direct-mail envelopes. The headlines on these buckslips read something like this:

> **If you've decided not to take advantage of this offer right now, please read on. . .**

This is the last kick at the cat, your last opportunity to turn a no into a yes. The copy on these slips would make one last offer or use one more argument in order to try to save that sale. Billions of these slips must have been printed, and millions of sales will have been saved as a result. Are there opportunities to try the same idea online? Yes, but you need to be careful. The most literal translation of a buckslip in the online environment is the use of a pop-up window. And while the paper buckslip was passive, the pop-up is very active and very intrusive. It interferes with what the user is trying to do. As a result, pop-ups that say "Are you sure you want to abandon your shopping cart?" will usually simply irritate your users. However, there are times at which you can try the same device in a passive format.

At Wilsonweb.com you are invited to subscribe to a paid-for newsletter. There is plenty of information provided that is both informative and persuasive—and plenty of opportunities to click a link through to the sign-up page. But if you get to the end of that first information page without clicking through, there's a link that says:

> **Read this only if you've decided not to subscribe**

That link takes you to another page that serves the same purpose as a buckslip, dishing up a few more compelling reasons to subscribe right now. Will this buckslip page change the minds of people who have decided not to subscribe? No, it won't. But it may work with some of those people who would quite like to subscribe and need that little extra nudge or piece of information to help them make up their minds.

Customers often come to your page wanting to make a purchase. They have questions and reservations, but they still want what you're selling. Your job is to answer the questions, peel away the doubts, and leave them feeling completely at ease about moving forward. The concept of the buckslip, however you choose to execute it, can help convert a few more people by providing some extra nuggets of information and some additional reassurance.

Don't Stand in the Way of Simple Actions.

It's hard enough to get people to take an action on your site, so don't get in the way of them doing so. A classic instance of impeding a visitor's actions is when you ask for more information than is required for the purpose. The request for action might start with something like this:

To sign up for our newsletter, click here.

An uninspiring line, but simple. From that link one might expect to be taken to a page where you are asked for the following:

Your email address _____

In truth, that's all you need to know about your visitor. And if you keep things that simple, you'll probably maximize the conversion rate on that page. Can you get away with asking for more, right at the beginning? Yes, so long as your customers can immediately recognize that providing the answers will add value in their eyes. So the following could work out fine:

Your email address _____

○ HTML   ○ Text

○ Monthly   ○ Weekly

Providing answers to these options will clearly allow the user to receive information at a time and in a format that suits them best. But when the information requested is clearly for the benefit not of the user, but of the marketer, that is a different story.

Your email address _____

Sex: ○ Male   ○ Female

Age: ○ 18–24   ○ 25–34   ○ 35–44   ○ 44+

Many users will feel an internal resistance to providing answers to these more personal questions. It's not that you should never try asking the questions at some point, if those answers are important to you and your marketing efforts. But don't ask them at this stage. It's presumptuous. You're getting too personal too early in the relationship. It's taken a lot of time, money, and effort to get that pair of eyeballs focused on your email or newsletter sign-up form. Why jeopardize that? Why do anything that might get in the way of persuading that person to provide you with his or her email address and permission to use it? Once the relationship is given that first spark, you will have plenty of time to follow up with additional questions at some later time. Whatever the action you want your users to take, make sure that you're not doing anything to stand in their way. Make it simple and worry-free.

To Become More Interactive, Think Like a Direct Marketer.

The Internet is a wonderfully responsive and interactive environment in which to do business. If you haven't come from a direct-marketing background, you may not recognize just how responsive the Web can be. On the flipside of that, if you do come from a direct-marketing background, you may not see that in the online world, responsiveness cuts both ways. Yes, your prospects will find it easy to respond to your offers—but they will also expect you to be responsive to their questions and interests. This is a shared space with shared responsibilities.

The Web can and should become the home of a more highly evolved state of direct marketing. Direct marketers should use all their existing skills in order to generate more online sales. But they should also see the huge benefits to be enjoyed through listening to constant feedback from their prospects and customers. Direct marketers should become as responsive as they want their customers to be. They should listen carefully and adjust their messages and offers to be in line with what their customers are asking for.

Online, use the skills of direct marketing both to sell and to listen.

CHAPTER NINE

EMAIL—WHERE COPY IS KING

Write Emails That Really Connect with Your Readers

That instant when your customers open one of your emails represents the most critical moment in your online endeavors. This is where you have the opportunity to really communicate one-to-one. This is where you have your customers' complete attention, undistracted, even if only for a moment. This is where you can touch them, as individuals, in a place that is entirely their own—their email inbox. This is where what you say and how you say it will set the tone for the future of your relationship with each and every customer.

Your Web site may carry the content of your business, it may be where you showcase all your products or services, but email is where you get up close and personal with your customers. This is a place where you can contain a reader's attention within a very narrow field. On your site, visitors can take a large variety of paths through your various pages and be exposed to numerous images and messages in goodness knows what sequence. You have very little control over the flow of the messages on your site. But in an email you can focus in on one point, one subject, one product, and one message. And you can control the presentation of that message from beginning to end.

What Makes the Email Inbox So Compelling?

Your customer's email inbox is where everyone wants to be. Why? Because that's where your customer's attention is directed most often. While a typical Internet user may visit an ecommerce site from time to time, perhaps once a week or once a month, that user will usually check out his or her inbox several times a week. And when users go to their inbox, it's with anticipation, in the hope that they'll find something they really want to read. Personal emails from friends and family are the ones that most people look for first, but that state of mind, that eagerness, can also carry over into emails from companies that they like to hear from.

Also, email has been around for longer than the Web or the Internet. Early email usage was the primordial soup from which life online emerged. This was where much of the language of the online world emerged. It's from here that everything else developed and grew.

Wag the Web Site.

An interesting exercise in understanding both your Web site and your email programs is to reverse them in terms of which came first. For the most part, people build sites and then figure out an email program that will drive repeat traffic and generate more business through their site. But turn that around for a moment. Imagine how your site would have turned out if you had first developed an email program and then spun out your Web site, based on the demands and needs of your emails.

In particular, consider the impact that would have had on the text you use on your site. The language one uses in emails is much more personal, much more conversational. And rightly so. But as soon as a reader clicks on a link in that email and is delivered to a destination page on your site, the tone and style of language usually changes significantly. Is this a good thing? Does it work to your advantage to switch voices between the two channels? Perhaps it does to some degree, because of the different roles that each channel fulfills. But that voice should probably not differ to the degree that you'll find between most emails and their destination sites. In the email, you are engaging readers in a very personal way, on their own terms. So why would you want to lose that proximity, that intimacy, just because you've moved those readers from your email to your site?

How you write your emails should be taking up a great deal of your attention. Nowhere else will you get closer, or be able to develop a more genuine sense of relationship, than in a customer's inbox. This is where you need to use your smartest writing skills, based on your very best understanding of who your customers are and what they want from you. And once you have found the right approach, that voice and delivery that best connects with your readers, consider applying some of that key learning to the pages on your Web site. You'll learn faster and smarter through email. Just be sure to apply that learning throughout.

The Proximity and Sincerity of the Language of Email.

The closer the person to whom you are talking, the more your language will approximate that of talking across a table, one-to-one. Online, the closest you'll come to true one-to-one is instant messaging or its "live-help" equivalent. Next comes email. It's not as immediate or as interactive as speech or instant messaging, but it's still the place where a more oral style of writing will serve you well.

In addition, the closer you are to the reader, the greater the need to be absolutely sincere and genuine. When you watch a TV commercial, you accept a certain amount of bending the truth. (No, your partner probably won't come dancing down the stairs, dying to tell you how soft and comfortable his or her clothes are after being washed in brand X.) But face-to-face, everyone expects much higher standards of honesty. And the same goes for email.

In trying to connect with customers, attempts that can be recognized as artificial just won't cut it. Here's an example:

Celebrate Passover and Easter at Indigo!

Perhaps you observe the eight-day celebration of Passover, enjoying the special foods of the Seder and sharing the story of Pesach. Or maybe you gather family and friends together for a delicious Easter dinner and anxiously await a visit from a certain bunny.

However you celebrate the coming of spring, Indigo wishes you and your family the very best.

1) Hunt for Fantastic Spring Savings!

From April 7–15 in all our store locations, we'll be offering 10–80% off over 100 great books, gifts, music and garden items— you just need to find them. Happy Hunting! To locate a store near you, click here. http://www.indigo.ca/Info/storeLocations.html

The email opens by making a guess that everyone in the audience is either Jewish or Christian. Safe ground? Not at all. What about those customers who are neither Christian nor Jewish? Are they not welcome? In addition, once you get past the first paragraph in this email, it becomes clear that those first sentences were simply a device to catch your attention. None of the items being offered for sale have any connection with Passover or Easter.

A device like this might possibly slip past the radar of your readers if this were the opening to a direct-mail letter, printed on paper, or even on your site. The experience is not nearly as intimate as with email, so some readers might let you get away with this. But not in their email inbox. And besides, why risk excluding or puzzling even one reader when you can write an introduction that would work much harder anyway?

It's important to recognize that the proximity of email brings both benefits and dangers. The key benefit is your ability to connect with your audience on a more personal basis. But the danger is that when you get up that close, they are far more likely to recognize any attempts at manipulation or deception.

Basic Inbox Survival Skills— Surviving the Glut

The need to get it absolutely right increases day by day. It's not just that everyone is receiving more and more emails from companies online; it's that most of those emails are intrusive, unwelcome, and uninvited.

When that happens, when customers feel that the majority of emails they receive are uninvited, it poisons the pool. The email inbox, once that most personal of places, becomes clogged with messages people simply don't want to read. When that happens, your customers will start applying their own sets of rules to determine which emails they'll read and which they will ignore or send to the trash.

Of course, this screening process is made harder for both the customer and any legitimate merchant because of the scarcity of information available in the inbox window itself. Basically, you have two small snippets of text to work with, the "From" text and the "Subject" text. And how you make use of these is often determined by staying one step ahead of the spammers who will try any trick available to get their messages opened.

For instance, there was a time when using a real name in the "From" box made a lot of sense. Instead of using "customersupport@domainnname.com" people were trying variations like "camilla@domainname.com" or simply "Camilla Jones." Using a real name made the email feel more personal, more appropriate to the space. If your name is very well known to your audience, your own name or that of a well-recognized spokesperson for your company can still work extremely well for you. But if the name isn't well known, your email could be mistaken for spam. More and more spammers are using bogus personal names in the hope that their email will be mistaken for a personal correspondence. (From there on, for the spammers, the math kicks in. They know that they'll get a minuscule response rate, but so long as the numbers are high enough and the cost of acquisition is low enough, they know they'll make a few bucks.)

So your best bet in the "From" line is simply to be sure that your company name is clearly shown. If you have a half-decent relationship with the recipient, your company name alone should be sufficient to get you at least a glance. If not, whatever you say in the email probably won't make too much of a difference anyway.

The second spot in which you can catch and hold the reader's attention is in the "Subject" line. Again, what works and doesn't work in this space has been limited by the spammers. There was a time when the "Subject" line could work powerfully when you identified it as being part of an ongoing correspondence. "As per our conversation."

"As requested," and even the use of "RE:" at the beginning of the "Subject" line all indicated this was just the latest in a series of emails, back and forth. Now that the spammers use all these and other lines as a way to fool their victims, you'll have to be careful how you use them.

Again, your best bet is simply to identify the source of the email once again—usually through your company name —and also to give some hint about why this particular email should be opened. If it's a newsletter that the recipient requested, identify it as such:

> Subject: "Company Name" newsletter, July

If the email is part of a program to which the customer has opted-in, make that clear:

> Subject: "Company Name" Sales Special—as requested

In this instance, the "as requested" phrase will work because it is preceded by your company name. (Of course, if that customer didn't expressly request that you send sales updates, you'll be shooting yourself in the foot with this message.)

Whichever way you choose to write the "From" and "Subject" lines for your emails, keep an eye on what the spammers are doing. Be aware of when their tricks and devices come close to or overlap the phrases and approaches you use yourself. When that happens, you'll need to make some adjustments or run the risk of your emails being mistaken for spam.

Of course, if future legislation manages to significantly reduce the amount of spam that is sent to people, this whole problem may go away. But in the meantime, be aware that the personal and proximate nature of people's inboxes is being continually muddied by the influx of uninvited garbage.

This Is Where You Need Character.

When inboxes fill up with spam, near-spam, and "I-can't-remember-whether-I-asked-for-this-stuff-or-not," it's time to wish that you, your company, and your emails had a strong, distinctive character. Character will always separate you from any crowd—at work, at social events, at home, and in email. A distinct, sometimes off-beat, and attractive voice with presence will usually catch people's attention.

Here's an example of a newsletter with fairly dry content, but a strong voice:

DAVENETICS . . . . connecting the dot coms*

March 19, 2001

{the official newsletter of the next five minutes}

subscribe at: (http://www.davenetics.com)

MONDAY AFTERNOON FIX

NOT WAITING BY THE INBOX —

The internet-age promise of more seamless access to your government representatives has run into a slight wrinkle. Too much email. Last year, members of Congress received more than 80 million messages. How do they handle the influx? Pretty much just how you would imagine. They hit the delete button. Funny, they don't seem to have any problems wading through all those forms being emailed to the IRS. The problem of email overload is one not limited to public officials. Email use has gone through the roof, but the tools to manage it have remained fairly static.

The Davenetics newsletter, written by Dave Pell, is simply a daily collection of links to interesting stories for his audience of people in the Internet industry. The content is dry, but the presentation is given character through the unmistakable voice of Dave himself. That one line—"{the official newsletter of the next five minutes}"—speaks volumes about both Pell and his approach to the Internet industry. It's also something of an inside joke for anyone doing business online, as an allusion to how quickly things change. A successful inside joke can work wonders, because it bonds the writer and his or her readers. The writer is "one of us." And when you're one of us, you can be sure that you'll get preferential treatment in the inbox.

Adjust the Length to the Purpose.

There are constant discussions about the appropriate length of copy for emails. And there is no definitive answer. The simplest rule for copy length in an email is to say enough to get the job done, but no more. And the key here is to determine and to understand exactly what the job is—*before* you begin writing.

An email may have just a single purpose. It may be to drive someone to a particular place on the Web. It may be to help build the relationship between the company and the recipient. An email may be delivered automatically in response to some action that the recipient has taken at your Web site. It may be a customer service email relating to a purchase.

If an email has more than one principal purpose, you may want to ask yourself whether that's such a great idea. Email is perhaps the first commercial communications medium known for which there is no budgetary pressure to include a long laundry list of promotional messages in every communication. In the world of print ads, direct mail, and other high-cost media, writers are frequently asked to mention as much as possible because of the cost of delivery. In other words, in the minds of some people in the marketing department, if it costs this much to deliver the message, let's make sure that as much ground as possible is covered in the space or time available. With email, this shouldn't be an issue, because the cost of delivery is so low.

So keep it simple. One purpose per message. And write in the knowledge that your customers' email inboxes are getting fuller and fuller and that their time and attention is becoming scarcer and scarcer. If they come to know you as a time hog who buries the meat of the message within lines and lines of unnecessary chatter, they'll soon learn to ignore your emails when they see the subject line. But if you are respectful of their time and attention, and deliver information that is truly of value to them, they'll come to appreciate your brevity and return the favor by giving each of your emails a quick read.

However, just to complicate things, being too brief with your message may result in a lost opportunity. Even if you cover just one point with admirable brevity, it makes sense to also use that moment to build and defend your relationship with your customers. So even an email that acknowledges an order placed at your site might contain a few words that make that customer feel comfortable with his or her purchase. And certainly, a customer service email should do more than just answer the question posed by your customers —it should also make them feel that their questions are welcomed and that their interest is valued.

Here's an example of how the answer to a simple question can be used as an opportunity to seed the beginning of a relationship. The question posed at this company's site was, "Do you ship to Canada?"

Dear John,

Thank you for writing to www.sportchalet.com

Unfortunately, because of distribution restrictions placed upon us by the manufacturers whose products we sell, we are unable to ship merchandise to addresses outside of the United States, including Guam, Puerto Rico, Samoa and the U.S. Virgin Islands.

We certainly apologize for any inconvenience this may cause. We will be re-evaluating this service in the near future. Please don't hesitate to contact us if you have any questions. Have a great day.

Please let us know if there is anything else we can do for you, and thank you for shopping at www.sportchalet.com

Sincerely,

Etc. . . .

In addition to answering the question, some effort has clearly been taken to demonstrate that the company would like to be able to serve John—even if it can't at this particular moment. So while the email is certainly longer than was necessary to say, "No, we don't ship to Canada," the extra words would probably be welcomed by most readers even if they are a little dry and formal.

You can get the idea more clearly by contrasting that last message to this one, in answer to the same question:

Dear John:

Thank you for contacting Burpee.

I'm sorry but we do not send catalogs or products outside the United States Postal Service

Thank You

It answers the question quickly, but without any warmth attached.

Using Email to Generate a Direct Response.

Email is a terrific medium through which to generate a direct response, because the manner of responding is so simple. In the offline world, responding to an offer or invitation of some kind usually involves at least a pen, a form, the purchase of a postage stamp, and a trip to the mailbox. That represents a lot of obstacles between that moment of thinking, "Maybe I'll check this out," and actually acting on that thought. But online, with email, one click of a link brings you to a destination page on a Web site. This, by far, is the simplest link between the first and second part of a two-stage sell ever devised.

Here's an example of how an email from an online retailer can quickly move customers from their email windows to your Web site:

Gwen's now has Foam Fun Clocks for the children, and they make great gifts too:

Stand Up Foam Clocks:
http://www.gwensjewelry.com/rc/funclock.htm

Large Wall Foam Clocks:
http://www.gwensjewelry.com/rc/funclock2.htm

Standard Wall Foam Clocks:
http://www.gwensjewelry.com/rc/funclock3.htm

** 70% off on these fine Gold Earring sets:
(1st come, 1st served—low quantities)
http://www.gwensjewelry.com/sale/sale1.htm

** 70% off on these "soup to nuts" items:
http://www.gwensjewelry.com/clearance.htm

** Every day is Father's Day—check these:
http://www.gwensjewelry.com/mom/mom5.htm

** New: we are now the distributors for these high quality Artistic and Religious stainless glass panels—Beautiful!

Other than some housekeeping information at the end of the email, that was pretty much it. No salutation, no chitchat. Just a series of simple links from the email to the Web site, with a very brief description of the products in question.

For lovers of foam clocks and gold earrings, this makes for a simple, brief email. And the clickthrough, rate is probably very reasonable. That's the beauty of emails that open with direct links to a site. Place those links in front of lots of interested customers and you'll get a good number of people checking out those pages on your site.

But has an opportunity been missed here? Possibly. There are two other things that this email might have done. One is to take the opportunity to use the message to cement the relationship with the customer. That message was pretty cold. No warm fuzzies. A greeting or salutation might have been nice. The other missed opportunity was to presell the destination page, or the offer, a little more before sending the reader away from the email.

When you capture people's attention through email, you can contain their focus and presell them on whatever it is you're hoping to sell at your site. But the moment they click that link and arrive at your site, they will be in a place with numerous distractions. Instead of looking at the one item or range of items you are hoping to sell, they might wander off elsewhere on the site, driven by a curiosity to browse and not by the intention to buy. But if you spend a little more time preselling within the far more contained and linear environment of an email, your conversion rates at the site might end up significantly higher.

Through the wonder of hyperlinks, emails are wonderful places through which to drive direct responses. Just be aware of the state of mind of your readers and don't send them away or lose them too early within the sales process.

Features, Benefits, and Then Some.

This is a copywriting and sales lesson that is as old as the hills, but still true and very often ignored by writers online. This lesson is particularly pertinent to how you handle both copy and hyperlinks in your emails.

The features and benefits argument goes like this. First, sell with benefits and then cement the sale with features. For instance, if you're selling a PDA, first pitch the benefits— that's where you connect with what they want rather than with what they need:

> New in town and need a map? Want to look up some contact information while you're on the go? Need to check some figures while you're in a cab on the way to that presentation? Want to look at photos of the kids when you're stuck in a hotel, far from home?

These are all benefits of having a PDA, presented as questions in order to engage the imagination and involvement of the reader. So when people ask themselves why they need such a thing, these are the kinds of questions that come to mind. They are the reasons why people need a PDA.

Information on a PDA's features is a lot more factual and a great deal drier.

- 8 MB memory

- 10,000 addresses, 1,000 memos, 400 emails

- USB recharging HotSync cradle

- AC power adapter

This is the kind of information you need in order to be sure that you're making the right choice. But in truth, in your heart, you're probably pretty set with your decision before it comes down to checking out these features.

Using the traditional benefits-followed-by-features approach will set you up for a traditional sales approach. Your outbound email, in an abbreviated form, might look a little like this:

Dear John,

Keep in touch with colleagues—and your family—while you're away from your desk with an XYZ PDA!

Here are just some of the great features that will help you get organized and keep in touch . . .

• 8-MB memory

• 10,000 addresses, 1,000 memos, 400 emails

• USB recharging HotSync cradle

• AC power adapter

That's a pretty traditional approach. Opening with a simple benefit and following up with some features. But with email you can probably do better than that. Because email is such an immediate and personal medium through which to sell, you might want to get a little closer still to what really makes that prospect click.

To get that "closer" feel, think about how you would persuade your own spouse or significant other that you need a $500 PDA. "Honey, it will be great. This means I can catch up on my email on the commute. So I won't have to do that when I get home. I'll have more time to spend with you and the kids!"

In response to this line of arguing, if you're really lucky, your spouse will say, "Hey, great idea, go for it!"

So if you're targeting married people who might be in the market for a PDA, use the more conversational and relaxed tone of email copy to try something like this:

Dear Joanne,

Have you seen the latest, XYZ PDA? It's a thing of rare beauty!

If you'd like one, but haven't figured out how to persuade your significant other that it's an "absolute necessity," here's the ammunition you'll need.

* Honey, it's got wireless! You and the kids will be able to reach me any time!

* Honey, it's got maps—so we won't get lost when we go into town!

* Honey, I'll be able to work on my commute. That means more family time when I get home!

* Honey, I just love this thing! It would mean so much to me!

And if your significant other is a little on the geeky side, here's some more ammo . . .

* 8 MB memory

* 10,000 addresses, 1,000 memos, 400 emails

* USB recharging HotSync cradle

* AC power adapter

Your next step? Right here:

http://www.bloggspda.com?blahblah

Etc.

In essence, you're using the traditional benefit-and-feature approach, but taking it even further. Because email is such a personal medium, it allows you to talk to your audience in a much more familiar and intimate way. Be a friend and talk like a friend.

Will being more personal, more close-up, and more "pally" really work better in your area? Test it and see. Vary the tone, approach, and the details, one at a time, and see what happens.

As for the placement of that hyperlink, that's always a tough call. If you place or repeat the link closer to the start of the email, you'll likely increase the clickthrough to the site. But if people click through on the first or an early link, they'll arrive at the site only half-primed to make the purchase. The only answer here, once again, is to test the placement and number of links from the email to your site. And when you do that, you need to measure not the clickthrough, but the actual conversion to sales. Which placement worked better when it came to actually making a direct sale through that email?

Getting the Tone Right with Business-to-Business Emails.

If you can get closer to your customers through email in the business-to-consumer world, does that mean that you can try the same in business to business? Will a more conversational, familiar approach really work? Yes, it probably will.

Here's an email that is sent out to a dealership network by Eric Lupton of poolfence.com:

Committed to making your home a safer place for children.

Current Lead Time: 3 Working Days

Ladies and gentlemen, we are proud to announce the biggest thing ever in the pool fence industry.

It's big.

Real big.

Twice as big as anything you've ever seen before.

It's the Thirty Foot Section!

Lower cost per foot, less holes to drill, easier to manage, cheaper shipping . . . the benefits go on and on. Just think of it as the CBXTRA. (No, this isn't the model name. Don't worry.)

The Thirty Foot Section is now available for 48" and 42" heights, ALL colors, and the 30" pole configuration.

We still offer the 15' section, but to move forward with the future, try the Thirty Foot Section for your next job. You'll be VERY pleased.

Just designate thirteen poles with your order. CBX-13, BB-13, CX-13 . . . you get the idea. Now 13 is your lucky number!

And Remember: Do you want to win a bar bet? Ask a friend to identify the technical word for the slanted line used to divide fractions or the parts of a date, as in 3/4, or 10/20/42. Your friend will almost certainly never guess it.

You don't know what it is? I'd better tell you. The word is "virgule." But I'm sure that was your next guess.

Take care.

That's certainly a lot more casual than the language you'd find in a traditional business-to-business direct sales letter. Once again, the writer is taking advantage of the unique proximity of email. He's connecting more closely than he ever could with direct mail. He really is making friends as he does business.

Think About How Best to Use HTML Emails.

The use of HTML in emails has opened up a host of opportunities for online retailers. Finally, you can send images of your products right through to a prospect's email inbox. It's like having the best of both worlds—the immediacy and proximity of email with the graphic capabilities of a Web site. The temptation to use HTML email at all times is huge.

Even if you sell content and not products, HTML provides an opportunity to sell and display banner ads or sponsorship links. This opens up the opportunity to push weblike content into people's inboxes. Indeed, many companies do just that—pretty much duplicating the exact interface you'll find on their site.

This holds huge advantages for anyone trying to sell something you can see. A book, a camera, a bread-maker, a golf club, a starter motor, a backpack, and so on. Show the item or items in the email, use sales copy to build a strong sales pitch while in the closed environment of the email, and then provide a link for the purchaser to click directly through to the shopping cart on your site.

But despite all of its advantages, don't automatically jump at the HTML option without considering a couple of issues. The first issue is that of download times. An HTML email can make for quite a large file size, and chances are that most of the people on your email list will be on a dial-up connection with transfer speeds of 56k or less. If you are marketing to the geek crowd or to people at their place of business, then you can safely assume a higher penetration of broadband access. But if your audience comprises regular people at home, chances are that over 85 percent of them will still have a dial-up connection and may become irritated by large files appearing in their inboxes. The degree of irritation felt will depend on how big the file is, how frequently you send emails, whether you offer the option of a text version, and whether you offer an easy way to unsubscribe.

The second factor to consider is the very significant difference between a text email and an HTML email when it comes to their impact on the character of the communication. One of the strengths of email as a communications channel between companies and their customers is its personal, one-to-one nature. Email that is text-only taps into that most basic of all uses of the Internet—people connecting, sharing, and learning through their email programs. It's what people learn first when they get online and what they do most from that moment on. Text email is the cornerstone of online communications. When used wisely, text email enables companies to tap into the network on that same, individual, intimate level. As with the example from poolfence.com above, even a business-to-business email can feel personal, connecting one individual to another.

But you can't do that with HTML. HTML emails don't come from people; they come from the marketing department of a company. The communication is no longer truly one-to-one. It's corporation-to-one. Can an HTML email still be personalized? Yes, but when you're looking at personalized emails that come with graphics, that personalized element is usually generated by some high-end software. It's personalization, but it's no longer personal in the way that a simple text message can be.

With HTML you lose the simplicity and innocence of email. With HTML the recipients know that they are being sold to. They know it's a pitch. But with text, if you're truly sincere in matching what you offer to what your customers want, and if you write in a genuine and personal style, you can still communicate in a way that really is one-to-one.

At the end of the day, it's up to you to determine the needs of your program. If the primary purpose of your emails is to shift units or generate advertising revenues, then HTML is the way to go. But if you can do without the generation of graphics in your emails and your plan is the growth of long-term relationships with some staying power, stick with text.

Don't Forget the Headline.

Should emails have headlines? Yes, they probably should. It's true that emails in the wild, in their natural environment, passing between individual users outside of commerce, do not have headlines. However, within the commercial environment a headline of sorts is very necessary.

First, a strong headline can make up for the fact that the announcement of an email in the inbox is limited to the very few and carefully chosen words that can fit into the "Subject" line. Given those restrictions, and given the very brief attention most emails will command, you'll need a strong headline to keep your readers reading.

You can also look at it as the equivalent of a Johnson Box in a direct-mail letter. The Johnson Box was invented by Frank Johnson, one of the best direct-mail copywriters of all time, during the late 1950s. The idea of the Johnson box was to capture the reader's interest before he or she even read the salutation or first line of the letter itself. Johnson was also the first person to take the P.S. on a direct-mail letter seriously. He noticed that readers often flicked through to the end of the letter and read the P.S. before anything else. So he started writing the P.S. as if it were a headline. And so has everyone else ever since. But the Johnson Box was just as important an innovation. Placed within a frame, or box, the text in this area was used to set up the letter that followed. Johnson used it to be provocative, to pique the reader's interest, to say a little, but not quite enough. Its purpose was to hold the reader's attention and interest long enough for the letter itself to begin to weave its magic. That may not seem like a huge innovation now, but at the time it was a significant break from what a letter "should" look like. And it worked extremely well.

You can apply that same thinking to the headline in your email. Use it as a hook to catch your readers' attention and intrigue them enough to keep them reading. Here's an example that works very well. It was sent by RedEnvelope.com a few weeks before Mother's Day:

Subject: It's all about Mom on May 13

Headline: Mother's Day is May 13
        Your mother says she doesn't want anything.
        Why start listening to her now?

The hope is that the subject line gets the email opened. After all, it's timely and was permission-based to a recipient who would recognize the RedEnvelope name in the "From" line.

Once the email is opened, it's up to the headline to hold the reader's attention and tempt her into reading on. This particular headline does a neat job of that because it touches on people's personal experiences as children, whatever their age now. Yes, moms always tell their kids not to get anything for Mother's Day, but the kids know that they should. And yes, the kids have spent years ignoring their mothers' perfectly good advice. By using copy that connects on a personal, emotional level, the writer succeeds in engaging the reader's attention. "Yes, you're talking to me. Tell me more." Following the headline is a selection of gifts that would be suitable for Mother's Day.

Here's an example of an email sent out at about the same time, also with its sights set on Mother's Day:

Put Mom in the Digital Picture!
April 25, 2001

Hello John!

Kodak is revolutionizing photography again—with the new KODAK DX3500 Digital Camera and EasyShare System! Now you can shoot a picture, touch a button and share your pictures with the world. Your pictures are automatically sent to your computer, ready for e-mailing and printing. Mighty. Simple.

With this example the attention we pay to the headline, such as it is, is diluted because the date comes immediately after it. "Put Mom in the Digital Picture!" would likely have worked better had it been given a little more white space around it after the date. But even if the headline had been given more prominence, it would ultimately have been a waste of effort because the body of the text makes no further mention of either mothers or Mother's Day. It's simply about cameras. It failed to deliver on the unspoken promise of the headline: "We'll solve your problem—we'll show you some great gift ideas that will make your mom happy on this special day."

This is a good illustration of how a headline can't work in isolation, but needs to be part of the broader message. The headline needs to open the door into a space that matches the opening.

Wine.com, in its pre-Mother's Day email, is quick to follow the headline with a series of linked subheads that continue and build on the headline's promise:

Great Gifts & Free Shipping for Mother's Day!

In This Email:

Need a Little Mother's Day Inspiration?

What's Hot: wine.com's Top-10 Selling Wines

Wine Team Picks: Spaghetti Wines

Special Offer From our Partner—Proflowers.com

This email doesn't connect with its readers in the same way that the RedEnvelope headline did, but it does recognize that the reader's attention is limited. Instead of involving them emotionally, it provides four quick links in the hope that one of these will attract their interest and keep them reading, and clicking.

Does every outbound email need a headline? No. And those that don't require any kind of headline introduction are those where the relationship between sender and recipient is at its strongest. But if your customers are fairly new to you and their attachment to your business is slight, then you may well need a strong headline to counter their first inclination to ignore your message. But further along in the relationship, when your customers come to recognize you as a source of value in their lives, you can back away from the powerful heading and work harder at presenting a very personal tone with your opening paragraph.

Be Specific about What's on Offer Early in the Email.

Writing an email is a story of lost eyeballs. You know that of the hundred thousand people who receive your email, only a small number will open it. The combination of the "From" name and the "Subject" line will fail to compel most readers to open the email.

Of those who do open the email, you know that you'll lose some at the headline and even more during the first paragraph. Remember, your customers' email inboxes are bulging with spam and near-spam. Even the most welcome emails are coming under close scrutiny. So once you've succeeded in persuading the reader to look at your email, that opening paragraph had better be good.

If you have the technology and a customer history to work with, you can make that first paragraph very targeted and very relevant. Like this one from Amazon.com:

> Dear John Smith,
>
> As someone who has purchased books by Terry Pratchett, you might like to know that his newest book, *Thief of Time*, has recently hit the shelves. You can order your copy at a savings of 20% by following the link below:

That's a very attractive invitation. John is being told about the arrival of a new title by an author he likes, and he gets to save 20 percent on the cover price at the same time.

By way of contrast, here's an example, still on the Mother's Day theme, that suffers from being totally nonspecific:

Dear Maclean's Reader,

Shop for your Mother's Day gift right now online! It's <u>easy</u> and it couldn't be more <u>convenient.</u> Simply <u>click here.</u>

The opening paragraph may be heavy on invitations to click, but gives no specific reasons to do so. This is an example of an opening that hopes and prays that the reader's own momentum will carry the reader through. Unfortunately, this is rarely the case. You're better off making a very specific and relevant offer and keeping your prose tight and to the point. Amazon.com did it by showcasing a single item that it was pretty confident would interest the reader. Wine.com did it by offering a choice of four specific links that moved the reader on. But to say, in effect, "Please, please click here" isn't going to get the job done.

Keep It Personal and Interesting as the Relationship Progresses.

It's tempting to focus too much of your attention simply on capturing a customer and making a good first impression with that welcome email. In truth, that first email is probably the most important one you'll ever have to write. But once the beginnings of the relationship are put in place with that first contact, you can't just turn your back and expect that relationship to grow on its own. It has to be built little by little. So it makes no sense to write a welcome email that is warm, conversational, and engaging if every email that follows is flat and cold. Whatever you promise in that first email, in both substance and tone, you need to deliver on, long term. That means paying as much attention to the fifth and fiftieth email as you did to the first. That first email may have opened like this:

Dear John Smith,

It's great to have you on board! Thank you very much for signing up for our weekly specials email. You can be sure I'll be
working hard to bring you some terrific deals.

So the fiftieth email shouldn't be like this:

Dear John Smith,

This week's specials are:

1. etc, etc

If John is still paying attention after 50 weeks, he
deserves better than that:

Dear John,

It's a special day today! This is the fiftieth email we've sent you
in this series and it's time for us to say thank you for staying
with us. Click on the link below for a free $25 gift certificate,
etc., etc.

Not only is the tone the same as that of the first email, but
the content recognizes the stage and level of your relationship. An outbound email system will often send out the same
message to the entire database. Even when that's not the
case, do you segment your list based on the length of time
that subscribers have been with you? If you're trying to
increase the loyalty of your customers, be sure that your
messages are adjusted to reflect the maturing nature of the
relationship.

Allow For and Welcome Responses.

Email is an interactive medium, and people expect to be able
to reply to the emails they receive. But does your company
want replies to its promotional emails? Are you even set up
to deal with them?

Putting aside the mechanics and cost of handling replies, when you welcome interaction with your readers, it forces you to rethink your whole approach and tone. Here is the final paragraph of an email from SmarterLiving.com:

> SECOND, if there is anything we can ever do better, please contact our customer service team at feedback@smarterliving.com. Ideas for new newsletters? Ways we could present the information better? New benefits you want to see? Suggestions? Please let me know. Thank you again for joining. I look forward to hearing from you.
>
> Sincerely,
> Dan Saul
> President and Founder
> Smarter Living

When you ask for the involvement of your readers, you are forced to write in a style that is personal and engaging. Corporate-speak won't work if you want to involve people in a real dialogue.

This is just one illustration of how the attitude behind your marketing will determine the style of your copy. If your attitude toward your customers is to take their money and keep them at a distance, your writing style will likely reflect that. But if your sincere intention is to listen to what your customers think and feel, then a more personal writing style will inevitably follow.

CHAPTER TEN

THE LANGUAGE
OF PERSONALIZATION

If the Language Isn't Personal,
Then Neither Is the Message

The technology of personalization has made remarkable advances over the last few years. Faster processing power, cheaper data storage, and increased access to customer information over the Web have led to an explosion of knowledge about customers and surfers online.

In theory, all this information could be used to deliver a remarkably personal experience to people using the Web—the ultimate one-to-one experience. So it's a little surprising when people find that a piece of direct mail on their kitchen counter is often just as personal as the email they receive through their computers. In fact, the familiar feel of that seemingly unwelcome rectangle of direct mail can often come a great deal closer to connecting with its audience on something approaching a human level.

If companies online know so much about everyone, why do their emails appear to be so impersonal? One answer to this question is that personalization software knows you by your data and not as a person. When this happens, the emails you are sent are directed to your "data points" and not to yourself. The software does a terrific job of crunching the data and letting a dotcom company know what to say to a particular person and when to send it. But all that new technology can only take the company to within about one arm's length of the customer. The technology itself can't deliver a personal message. Only a person can do that. That gap, that one arm's length, is proving to be quite a distance.

In short, personalization will never feel personal unless there is some element in there that touches you on something approaching a human level. That one element can be created by good writing.

To Get Started, First Heal the Disconnect between Your IT Staff and the Marketing Department.

In many companies online there is a distinct disconnect or fracture between the people in the IT department and the people in the marketing department. Different budgets, different power bases. But one thing is for sure when it comes to delivering outbound messages through the Web and by email: Nothing will get achieved without the full cooperation of the IT people.

The division between IT and marketing runs deeper than just within the online companies that are looking to sell their goods and services. That division also exists within the software companies that create and sell the personalization "solutions."

In the words of Jack Aaronson, director of personalization at Barnes & Noble.com:

> One of the big problems is that vendor companies tend to spring up from one of two fountains: research people or marketing

people. This is why you find two types of software out there: software that is accurate, precise, fast, and well-designed, but doesn't solve any of your business problems; or, software that solves all of your business problems poorly.

Why? Well, the schism between marketing and tech is huge, they don't talk to each other, and moreover, don't feel like they need to. So, they end up solving the wrong problems, or implementing a feature without really understanding it, making the "next version" that the marketing people had in mind nearly impossible, because it wasn't implemented to scale in that direction. Having worked for a vendor on both the technical side and the marketing sides, I can attest to this first-hand.

So there's a problem. Even if the marketing people and their IT counterparts in the ecommerce company were close and cooperative, their efforts could be undermined if there were divisions within the company that created and then sold them the personalization software they depend on.

Almost every dotcom company uses personalization or CRM software to deliver pages and emails to its audience. The efforts of the company can be seriously undermined when marketing and IT are not working in harmony. This simply underlines the damage that is done when the marketing function is looked down upon. When marketers and copywriters are accorded insufficient respect, the technology runs rampant and delivers messages that simply don't connect with customers.

If the Writing Isn't Personal, Then Neither Is the Message.

Here's an example of an email sent to someone who asked to be put on the Victoria's Secret mailing list. After the sign-up acknowledgment email, here is the first marketing email that was sent out:

Dear Preferred Client,

Welcome to Victoria's Secret E-mail—exclusive e-mail news!

Now that you have signed up to receive our special mailings, you'll be the first to hear about exciting new fashion and media events, special online promotions and more. These exclusive e-mail updates will be sent to you as exciting new events unfold (about twice a month).

Is "Dear Preferred Client" the very best they could do? And was the recipient really meant to be delighted by the prospect of receiving "exclusive e-mail news"? The tone is reminiscent of a style of direct-marketing writing that was current back in the 1980s. In the eighties you might have been flattered to consider yourself a "preferred client" of American Express, for example. And you might even have believed that the news the company was sending you was "exclusive." But not today, not through email. Not online.

How can you be a preferred client if you have only just signed up? And how can the simple act of signing up entitle you to anything exclusive? It's clear that everyone who signs up will receive the same treatment. There's nothing exclusive about it.

That final sentence quoted above, "These exclusive e-mail updates will be sent to you as exciting new events unfold (about twice a month)," indicates a certain misunderstanding of the online environment. Email is uniquely fast and simple. It carries millions of fresh and spontaneous ideas and messages between individuals every day. But now Victoria's Secret is going to use this medium to send you emails "as new events unfold" according to a predetermined schedule—"about twice a month"? Planned spontaneity?

This approach to copywriting works in the world of direct mail only because the medium belongs to the messenger. Companies buy and own that channel of communication, and they reach each customer or prospect in a state of splendid isolation. Offline, customers open their direct-mail envelopes alone. They are isolated and unconnected. Under these circumstances you can tell them that they are on an exclusive list and they'll believe you. Tell them they are preferred clients and you'll manage to fool some of the people most of the time. But online, with email, you're working within a shared environment. When you're full of it, everyone can see.

So why would a company as successful as Victoria's Secret send out an email like this? How could a company with such a beautifully defined and expertly crafted brand send out an email that does nothing to build that brand, but actually spends it? How could the company sound so wrong?

The likely answer is that it is making the same mistake as so many other companies online. It is investing its time, money, and efforts into every aspect of doing business online, with the exception of what it takes to cross those last two feet between the technology and the customer. It's investing in the technology of message delivery, but not in the messages that are being delivered.

What You Lose When You Fail to Be Personal with Those First Few Emails.

A failure to be personal does the most damage at the very beginning of what you hope will become a fruitful relationship.

First, consider the cost of getting prospects to the point where they'll sign up at your site. Maybe they're not going to buy something right now, but they've invited you to keep in touch. You've received permission. There's a considerable cost involved in getting a prospective customer to this stage.

It may be $10, or it may be $100 or more—depending on your business and model.

But once you have someone's email address, you really do have an opportunity to become personal. There's only so far you can go to make your site pages one-to-one, but now that you have that person's email address and have been invited by him to appear in his inbox, you have the makings of a profitable relationship—for both parties. He gets the products or services he wants, and you get to transact some business.

This is a unique moment and should not be squandered. It certainly shouldn't be the time you choose to greet your customer with "Dear Preferred Client." It's at this point that you need a great copywriter. Someone who really understands the moment and its value and purpose. Someone who can clearly understand what is important to the reader at that moment. What can be said that will be reassuring? What can you say to make your customers feel they can trust you? What will make them smile? What will make them anticipate your next email with enthusiasm?

This moment when a company online comes face-to-face with an individual customer seems to throw many corporations into a state of confusion. That said, some companies get it absolutely right. Here's the opening to the first email you receive after signing up at Drugstore.com:

Dear John,

Welcome to drugstore.com!

We want you to have a great experience using our service. Our goal is to take the chore out of drugstore shopping, and to make your life easier by offering:

• Home delivery and 24-hour ordering, seven days a week

• Three times as many products as your average drugstore

- Complete privacy and confidentiality
- Online access to our pharmacists, product information, and product reviews

These first few lines are packed full of benefits for the customer that underline the value of shopping with Drugstore.com. The fact that the company uses the space to talk about what it is offering its customers speaks volumes about the company.

It's the Online Environment That Really Puzzles Many Corporations.

Companies don't feel confused at all when they are talking to millions of people at a time. Take a look at what QVC does when it sells products by TV. Millions of loyal fans will sit by and watch trusted QVC hosts as they talk about and praise the latest product on sale. QVC really does look into every product carefully before making a recommendation, and the hosts really are known and trusted by millions of viewers who listen to them for advice on what to buy. Part of what makes QVC successful is that it has found a way to build trusted relationships through the most massive of mass media.

Companies may know how to earn their customers' trust over the TV, when they are selling one-to-ten million. And they may also be able to do the same, one-to-one through the mail—where Victoria's Secret excels with its catalogs. But it's a whole different story when it comes to email.

In this arena, where companies need to communicate one-to-one over the most broadly shared and immediate communications medium ever devised, they stumble. They have yet to figure out how they can present themselves in a "personable" way.

David Weinberger, of *The Cluetrain Manifesto* fame, talks about zero-to-one marketing. Companies like to talk about how they practice one-to-one marketing. The first "one" is the company, and the second "one" is the individual customers. Mr. Weinberger takes issue with this notion because the company often doesn't qualify as a "one." It's not one-to-one—it's large corporation-to-one. Or as he so simply puts it, zero-to-one.

Don't Be Fooled by the Siren Call of Automation.

Ananova.com is home to "the world's first virtual newscaster." In addition to reading news stories, you can also hear the news being delivered through the voice of Ananova, a computer-generated, animated female head. Ananova looks like she's escaped from a family-rated video action game. She has short hair, a pleasant face, is vanilla flavored, and talks with a computer-generated voice. She'll never offend anyone and is completely devoid of character.

Imagine QVC trying to replicate its success on TV by creating a trusted host through computer animation. Instead of a real person in front of the camera, it would create a computerized host who would appear on a computer screen. Would QVC achieve the same success? Would the experience be as personal? Absolutely not. And this points to the greatest challenge that companies still face online—communicating one-to-one in an interactive environment.

The ideal solution to being truly one-to-one with an interactive medium like email is to hire and train as many frontline staff as it takes. Make sure they all have great writing skills and deal genuinely with every customer, one-on-one. For small companies, this is probably the best answer. Leverage the power of your computer systems, giving your email staff full access to customer files, but have the emails written by individual staff members. However, for larger companies this would be cost-prohibitive, even for high-value customers.

For Large Companies, the Answer Lies Not in Personalizing, but in Being Personable.

Your customers' email inboxes are highly personal and private spaces. It's where your customers hear from friends, family, and colleagues. At its best, email demands that the voice of your company be recognized as that of an individual. And that individual cannot talk in the safe voice of corporate-speak.

Jeremy Hiebert, the writer for the @*Bridges* newsletter, makes his voice unmistakably genuine and individual in a number of very creative ways. @*Bridges* is a newsletter aimed at young adults who need information on career planning. Here's an example of how he imparts information and touches on your funny bone, both at the same time.

> "Don't be afraid of hard work or getting your hands dirty," says Glenn Boyd, a plumbing apprentice. "There'll be times when you're up to your knees in a ditch full of mud, trying to lay pipe."

> PR Spinner: While these statements are true, you don't want to scare off potential plumbers by mentioning that you'll ever be knee-deep in anything. Good thing he used the word mud. You want to highlight the rewards and phenomenal growth potential of the field.

In this one article he tells it the way it is about choosing a career as a plumber. Then he follows each straightforward block of text with comments from the corporate "PR Spinner." What a great way to throw his own voice into context. Not only is he poking fun at the way in which career counseling is usually handled, but at another level he's also poking fun at the corporate-speak that pervades the Web. And guess which style and tone his audience of young adults prefers.

How does this relate to personalization? It does address the issue, but by flipping it on its back. Instead of the people at @*Bridges* trying to personalize and customize every email to every recipient, they take the reverse approach. Rather than trying to please everyone, they aim to become pleasing through their own, single character. They give their newsletter a voice and a definite character. They personalize it by being personal, by being distinct, by being themselves—and not by trying to be something different for every different reader.

Desperately Trying to Be Human.

With the best will, and the best PR spinners in the world, it's tough for a company to show its human qualities. This is particularly true of an online business, because almost every interaction with customers and prospects is preordained and automated by the backend of your systems. When such and such happens, this page will be served. When something else happens, an email will be triggered. Variable text selections in an email will be determined by matching the fields in a particular database.

In the days of ads and direct mail, at least a copywriter got to read the page, touch the paper, proof it at the printer's, and keep in touch with what was being said and sent out on a daily basis. However, when personalization software is plugged into the backend systems and the variable text choices and combinations have been selected and written weeks before, everything is hidden from human view.

From a copywriter's perspective, this is a nightmare. How can you write great text that is a pleasure to read and genuinely engages its readers when everything is being cut up, reconstructed, and finally written and delivered by a computer? Where's the soul in that? It's little wonder that personalized email often feels as personal as the instructions on your tax return. The technology is killing the purpose.

Picture in your mind the process of writing great copy that is personal, engaging, and effective in making a sale.

First, here's how copy gets written by Neil French, an irreverent, ridiculous, and hugely talented copywriter from the United Kingdom:

> Firstly, I get a good bottle of red: ideally, Rioja; possibly a Vega Sicilia or a Castillo Ygay, from the cellar, and remove the cork. Then I find a large expensive wine glass, of the type that goes "ting" for a long time after you've tinged it, and place that in close proximity to the bottle and myself. This takes years of practice to perfect, but persist; I think you'll find it worthwhile.
>
> Then I pour some of the wine into the glass and I think about the ad. Snatches of sentence, natty little phrases, excellent words, all come to mind. But I never write them down. All this while I am simultaneously drinking the red, slowly, from the tingy glass, (I warned you this was the tricky part), but I'm withstanding the temptation to pick up a pen. When I've finished the wine there frequently doesn't seem a lot of point in thinking about bloody ads any more, so I have a little lie down.
>
> When I wake up, I let rip. Anything that survives the little lie-down is obviously memorable, and goes in the ad. Anything I've forgotten obviously isn't and doesn't.
>
> Source: *The Copywriter's Bible*, AD & AD Mastercraft Series

Ridiculous, but hugely human. Now think of that email that is being written to go out to a particular segment of the database with 16 variable text elements. The writer sits at her PC and looks over at that sheet of paper that shows the many variable text fields and where they occur. Then our writer begins to write. What's at the top of her mind? "How the heck can I accommodate all these different variables and still end up with an email that sounds like it might have come into contact with a human being at some point?" Finally, our writer gives up, just writes the darned thing so it at least makes sense, and then consumes some cheap red wine out of a plastic cup and passes out.

If a key part of personalization is to be personal, copywriters are going to need some help, and the software needs to be designed with that end in mind. That is to say, if personalization software is designed to deliver personalized messages, then it also has to accommodate the act of writing those messages in a personal, human way.

When All Else Fails, Bypass the Systems.

When you can't get personal through existing systems, just avoid the systems.

Many years ago one of the major U.S. airlines sent out a Christmas season card to approximately 5,000 of its frequent fliers. Each envelope was addressed by hand, with a pen. A real postage stamp was used. On the card, the recipient's name was written in, by hand, with a pen, and was signed by four or five of the airline's employees. A traditional season's greeting was printed on the right-hand side. There was no response mechanism, no sales pitch, no phone number or return address on the card. It simply wished everyone a happy Christmas holiday in the most personal way that a large company could manage. In spite of the fact that there was nothing being sold and no response mechanism included, over 50 percent of the recipients either wrote to or called the airline to express their appreciation.

An exercise like that may be expensive, but the return on investment must have been phenomenal. In a world of automation, a highly personal touch still wins, hands down.

In the online world, you may want to take some of your emails outside of the automation loop. Write something truly engaging and personal that is about recognizing the reader and not selling your products. Something out of the blue. Something memorable. Something personal.

CHAPTER ELEVEN

SERVICE WITH A SMILE

The New Language of Customer Service

Customer service online. Here's a place of horrible conflict, both between customers and merchants and internally within the merchant organization. In fact, what makes the Web such an attractive place for both companies and their consumers also makes it a nightmare for customer service. Almost every aspect of customer service online leads to disappointed expectations.

First, your customers know the Web as a place where they can communicate with family, friends, and colleagues with incredible ease and speed—through email, instant messaging, and discussion lists. And it costs them almost nothing. People are connected, and they love the simplicity and immediacy of it.

Companies also love the fact that regular people like to connect and do things quickly online. So dotcoms send out millions of emails and then provide their visitors with a fast, convenient way to shop. The immediacy of buying online matches the immediacy of people's regular activities on the Web, and they like it.

The outcome? The outcome is that companies have built up an expectation of immediacy and an implicit promise of fast, personal service. The trouble is, companies can't deliver on that promise. They love the fact that they can blanket-email millions of people at just pennies a pop, but they hate the fact that those millions of people might want to talk back. In the good old days of print ads, billboards, and direct mail, companies could broadcast their messages and then sit back and wait for the dollars to start rolling in. They didn't have to worry about a significant number of people wanting to talk back, because to do so was inconvenient.

That's the double-edged sword of doing business online. You want to tap into a hugely connected population and sell your wares, but you don't want those people talking back to you. Unfortunately, it's not working out that way. Your customers are very comfortable in their interactive space and have some very reasonable expectations of the behavior of others in that space. A key expectation is that the questions they ask companies will be answered.

Three significant barriers stand in the way of delivering great customer service online.

The First Big Barrier to Great Customer Service Is Cost.

The ideal answer to handling customer service inquiries is to handle each one individually, one-on-one and very quickly. That's the customer expectation. And why not? The customer is thinking, "Hey, you can bill my credit card in a nanosecond, but you'll take a week to answer a simple question? What's with that?"

But here's why companies can't and won't answer every inquiry one-to-one, person-to-person:

Customer request	Cost per interaction
Telephone	$40 – $60
Email	$10 – $30
Collaboration	$2 – $10
Web self-help	$1 – $2

Source: *1 to 1 Quarterly*, Premier Edition

When customers have such easy access to your company through your Web site, they love to get in touch. And if your margins are slim, one such customer interaction can wipe out your profit on the transaction.

The cost creates an immediate internal conflict within any customer service group. The job of the customer service group staff is to do everything they can to keep their customers happy, but the more time they spend on a customer, the less likely it is that the transaction will be profitable. Agents are caught between a rock and a hard place.

When you consider this conflict, it explains why customer service phone numbers are often hidden a few pages deep within the site, or served up only once a customer starts placing items in the shopping cart. It's all part of a delicate balancing act—trying to meet customer expectations, but without spending too much.

The Second Big Barrier to Great Customer Service Is Lack of Trust.

One way to handle the larger volume of customer interaction that the online environment demands is to expand the ways in which individuals in your company are able to talk with your customers. In traditional organizations, interacting with customers is the job of the customer service department alone. That group of dedicated people may be within your building, or the job might be outsourced to a professional call center somewhere else. The call center agents are well trained and know exactly what to say, prompted by scripts and, it is hoped, the caller's history on the screen in front of them. Responses are carefully controlled, predetermined, and repetitive.

But online, some agents find the call of a more free-ranging style of conversation just too much to resist. One such agent was Jill Griffin of American Airlines. In addition to her regular work, she started corresponding with customers through the bulletin boards at Flyertalk.com, a site devoted to frequent flyers. She gathered quite a following of people who appreciated her frank and open nature. At first, American Airlines was supportive of her efforts. Then it became a little concerned about an employee representing the airline in an environment that was outside of its control. The next step was to ask her to add a disclaimer at the end of every post, saying that her opinions were not sanctioned by American Airlines. And finally it told her she just had to stop altogether.

It's unfortunate that Jill's employer couldn't have trusted her enough to continue. She was clearly doing a great job for the airline. And part of her appeal to the audience she collected together outside of work was her natural, unprompted, unorchestrated voice. Outside of work she was free to write naturally, in her own style.

The Third Big Barrier to Great Customer Service Is the Language.

Much of what made Jill popular as a spokesperson for American Airlines was, in all likelihood, the way in which she wrote. When you post a message to a discussion list, your style is going to be a lot more natural than the style you use at work, with supervisors pacing up and down the carpet behind you.

The language of traditional customer service does not sound right to the "ear" online. It's too structured, too carefully prepared, too cautious, and with too little promise. Worst of all, it's often impersonal.

But the biggest barrier of all when it comes to customer service online is the inability of traditional customer service agents to write as fluently as they speak. In the offline world, most customer service events take place over the phone. True, that's a ghastly experience in itself. The construction of confusing pathways through telephone hell will dissuade all but the hardiest or most desperate of consumers. But when a customer does get through to a customer service agent, they talk to one another in a fairly fluent manner.

Yes, the customer may be distressed or angry. Yes, the agent may sometimes be referring to prompts on a computer monitor. But they can still have a conversation. In fact, anyone who has completed a couple of grades at school can talk pretty much as fluently as the next person. But with the written word, it's different. Very few people can write as fluently as they can speak. And that's a problem online—where the majority of customer service interactions take place through email or live, text-based chat.

This is a problem, because text is the way in which customers like to interact online, in emails and instant messaging. People may not always be grammatically correct in what they say, but they get the message across without any trouble. Which brings us back to the issue of company control and lack of trust. In truth, any call center employee can have a good chat with a customer in text. But when these employees write, they'll be making the same grammatical errors as their customers. They'll be chatting away in the natural, easy way of online writing. That probably wouldn't be a problem for the customer, but it very often is a problem for the company. Companies don't want to be written about in a casual way. They don't want customer service agents making up company positions as they go along. They don't trust their employees enough to have them representing the official company voice.

Given this unease with the natural way in which their employees are able to write, companies all too often provide prewritten, preapproved text for their agents to drag and drop into the appropriate spots.

Beware the Automated Text . . .
Beware the Pretense.

Once you have that preapproved, drag-and-drop text, along comes the lure of automation. Companies automate their systems to do the dragging and dropping for them, or they automate their employees to do the same.

In the first instance, where that process is completely automated, emails will be generated by customer requests from a Web site. Here's a typical automated response:

> Thank you for your e-mail. At CircuitCity.com we are committed to providing excellent customer service. One of our Customer Service Representatives will respond by the end of the next business day.

There's no reference to the specific inquiry or event that triggered the email. This is a blanket communication that will suit any circumstance. The downside of a communication like this is that the customers will almost certainly be disappointed. They've emailed the company, they see a response come into their inbox, they open it, and . . . it's an automated message generated by a few lines of code. They had hoped for an answer and instead received a stalling tactic. What they had hoped would be contact with a human turned out to be contact with an autoresponder. Is an autoresponse better than no response at all? Probably. But couldn't the message have had a little more warmth? Something like:

> Thank you for your email. This is an automated response—just to confirm that we have received your message. One of us will get back to you in person as soon as we can. In fact, you can be sure of an answer by the end of the next business day.
>
> Best wishes,
>
> Janet Smith
> Your Customer Service Representative

It's still automated, but acknowledges that fact at the beginning. And it's from a person, an individual, not from an anonymous corporate entity. Although it doesn't answer the customer's inquiry, it at least touches the customer on something approaching a human, personal level.

In another circumstance, you might be responding to a customer inquiry and plan to use one or two prepared blocks of text as part of your reply. When the contents of your email messages are a mixture of new text and pre-prepared text, honesty is the best policy. Cynthia Currence, national vice president of Strategic Marketing & Branding for the American Cancer Society, describes ACS's approach:

> Our operators let people know ahead of time that part of the information they're including has been pre-prepared by the experts. So they get permission first, permission to drag and drop a piece of information that deals specifically with what they want.

This way you can turn a potential problem into a benefit. By declaring what you're about to do ahead of time, you remove any suspicion that you're trying to fool your readers. You're not trying to use technology to manipulate the readers into thinking that every word has been written specifically for them, one-on-one. Instead, you're saying, "Hey, I don't have all the answers personally, but here's the information we send out in response to that question. If you need to know more, be sure to let me know." Approach it this way and your customers get the warm feeling of dealing with a real person, plus the knowledge that they're being given information that's been put together by experts.

Beware of Live Help That Is Deceased.

Automation and the accompanying disappointment are even more prevalent in the area of live help through an online chat function. Typically customers on an ecommerce site will request live help through a small pop-up box that appears on the screen.

The advantage of live help to customers is that the response is either immediate or almost immediate. They don't have to wait until the end of the next business day. The advantage to the company is that it can reach the customer while he or she is still at the site—intent, it is hoped, on making a purchase. By being live, the communication can bring a great benefit to both parties.

The trouble is, live help, as a medium of communication, approximates to instant messaging. This is where people speak most freely and casually. By using a commercial equivalent of instant messaging, you're creating an expectation within your customers' minds. They'll expect instantaneous and spontaneous interactions with your customer support staff. Of course, this isn't what happens. A single live-help agent might be handling as many as five concurrent "conversations." Also, the agent will be answering a lot of the same questions, time and time again. And, of course, he or she will be answering all questions in a voice and manner approved by the company. How does the agent achieve this? Through the same process of dragging and dropping pre-prepared answers.

Dragging and dropping answers through a live-help window is oxymoronic. How can "live" help be dragged and dropped? Why disguise a perfectly good person as a computer?

Here's a real example of a short dialogue through a live-chat window:

John: Do you ship to Scotland?

Tracie: Here is a list of our Boutiques outside the USA. We can also assist you in placing your order in Europe, Canada and Japan. Please call us at 1-800-946-3482 if you would like assistance with placing your international order. Thank you!

Does that answer sound spontaneous? Not really. It only answers John's question indirectly, and it has the sound of "print." And, of course, it is. It has been dragged and dropped from a folder of prepared answers. Regular people who chat through instant messaging don't say things like, "We can also assist you in placing your order in Europe, Canada and Japan." That's corporate-speak. The live operator isn't there as a person who interacts with customers on a human level, but simply as a smart intermediary between the customer and an automated system.

Even if a large degree of automation is necessary to handle multiple inquiries at a reasonable cost, there are very simple ways in which you can make customers feel they are being dealt with on something approaching a human level. The addition of just a few words—the work of a few moments—could have made that message feel much more personal:

> Tracie: Sorry John—but I'm afraid we don't ship to Scotland. I wish we did! Here is a list of our Boutiques outside the USA. We can also assist you in placing your order in Europe, Canada and Japan. Please call us at 1-800-946-3482 if you would like assistance with placing your international order. Thank you!

That's simply another 14 words tacked on to the beginning of the message. No big deal. But it at least shows John that there is another person at the end of the line who really is reading his message and responding to it.

Anything Less Than a Human Voice Is Disappointing.

Almost by definition, your customers will turn to your customer service function only when their experience with your technology has frustrated them. They have tried to find what they want on your site or have tried to execute an action that attracts them, with disappointing results. It's when things go wrong that they seek out a customer service solution. At this point their hope is that they will not be faced simply with more technology, but will receive direct assistance from a living, breathing human being.

More often than not, online customers are disappointed by the customer service solutions they encounter. They reach out in the hope of connecting with a real person and end up being handled by another level of technology. At this point, disappointment often turns to frustration and anger.

Unfortunately, it is not realistic to expect that every customer inquiry can be handled immediately, one-on-one, by a highly trained and articulate customer service agent. But at the very least, every automated response should be *written* in such a way as to sound and feel human. Every block of customer service text, whether it was written for use in your email responses or for live chat, should be reviewed and improved. That text should carry the empathy and concern of a real person. It should be written in the language of a regular person, not in the starchy text of a marketing manual. It should touch and connect on an individual level. Customers who read that text should feel relieved and welcomed—not frustrated and rejected.

CHAPTER TWELVE

WRITING NEWSLETTERS

The Best Way to Hold Your
Customers' Attention

In the offline world, if you really want to punish a copywriter, ask him or her to write your company's marketing newsletters. Companies send their customers newsletters to promote sales, but disguise the whole mess as an advertorial of some kind. What's new. Upcoming services. Special deals. Most such newsletters end up as a weird synthesis of everything that is bad about commercial writing. No focus, too little character, too much political and departmental intervention, too little investment, and so on.

If you're looking for evidence that the Internet turns conventional marketing practices upside down, look at the difference between offline newsletters and the best of their online counterparts. In common with email, online newsletters grew out of the imagination of individuals, not the marketing divisions of large companies. Those early newsletters were evidence of passionate individuals finding a space in which they could self-publish their views and share their experiences with others. The Web is now home to tens of thousands of newsletters, most of which have only very small audiences. But a common thread that still runs through many of them is the passionate voice of one or two people who have something exciting they want to say, and are delighted to be able to do so via the Internet.

In the early days a newsletter was the place for editorial only. It might have contained links to sites of interest or even carried text ads as a means of supporting its costs, but it wasn't an ad. It was a soapbox, but not designed for selling soap.

Here's the opening to a recent newsletter that still carries the early ideals of how a newsletter should be:

Ah-choooo! Cyberheads, and Bless You, too!

We're just coming off April's Pollen Tour. Though minimal, we covered some serious real estate in the U.S. for some fabulous shows and sneezing. Thanks to all in the Southeast, New England (including a sell-out at The Somerville Theatre!) and our Lap o' Lake Michigan Tour (we've got the official U.P. bumper sticker on The Edshed to prove it).

In recent History, EFO has become enormous fans of the satirical Madison, WI-based rag "The Onion." In conjunction with our show in Madison—they actually gave us mention in their music column and were (thankfully) merciful and kind. If memory serves, the phrase "madrigal-fueled and sparkly" was used to describe us. Thanks?

This is part of the May issue of the official newsletter of the band Eddie from Ohio. No, they don't have a wall covered with platinum hits. But they do have a following, and they write a darned good newsletter. It's about them. It's about what they think. It's about who they are. And you'll notice from what they say and how they say it that they use this newsletter to speak to their fans. They say thank you. It's like a long letter home. The voice is clear and singular, the topics covered are wide and various, and the writers feel comfortable in the knowledge that their readers will be interested in all the news. Later in the newsletter they list the dates and venues of upcoming gigs. So there is a commercial benefit to their having a newsletter. But the text isn't heavy with self-promotion. It's light; it's fun; it's well written without being tight or stuffy. It's a classic rendition of the way so many newsletters used to be.

What's the bottom line here? The bottom line is that people will read this newsletter. And that's why companies online should pay attention to the benefits of good newsletters; they get opened and they get read.

The Difference between an Email and a Newsletter.

The difference between outbound email programs and newsletters is certainly becoming blurred around the edges. Ask many dotcoms what those differences are and they'll just shrug. But if you want to use newsletters effectively, you need to understand what makes them different.

A newsletter has a consistent publication schedule and is designed, primarily, to share information and knowledge in an editorial format. A commercial email is a great deal more intrusive. Its purpose is to solicit a direct customer action of some kind. The intent is to drive a sale, either immediately or at some future time.

If a commercial email is the equivalent of a direct-mail envelope in the bricks-and-mortar world, a newsletter is the equivalent of a magazine subscription. It may carry ads, but you still read it for the content.

Use Online Newsletters to Win Back Your Customers' Attention.

You can take advantage of the differences between an email and a newsletter to build stronger relationships with your customers. First, use your permission-based email programs to make sales and drive traffic. Make their purpose clear. Yes, add character. Yes, create a voice. But also, be forthright and honest about the purpose of these promotional emails. Their purpose is to drive readers to your site with a view to taking an action, whether that be to register, sign up, or make a purchase.

If you put the sales burden on the shoulders of your emails, that leaves you free to use a newsletter or two for a quite separate purpose—to engage, inform, educate, amuse, and delight. Do those things and you're well on your way to making friends with your customers, building deeper relationships, and further insulating them from predation by your competitors.

When you make your newsletter a pitch-free environment, you also help build trust between yourself and your customers. It's a competitive and busy environment out there, so it's a relief for your customers to be able to receive something of value from you without having to feel on the defensive or fight off a hard sell. While you may not see an immediate return on this process of building trust, it will have a very positive effect on building your brand in the medium to long term.

Give Your Newsletter a Purpose.

According to eMarketer, Americans were already receiving over 96 emails a week back in 2000. And that figure has been climbing ever since. As a result, your customers are becoming very picky over how they use their time and what they read. One of the keys to getting your newsletter read is to give it a clear purpose and offer a genuine value. Why would your customers read your newsletter? What's in it for them? This is the point at which you'll be thankful you decided to do the heavy promotions in your emails, leaving the newsletter free for building relationships.

Geoffrey Kleinman has been publishing *The Kleinman Report* since 1995, and it's still going strong. If you go to his site at Kleinman.com, you see that his report is described as follows:

> A free e-mail newsletter that will change the way you use the Internet. Featuring: important Web sites, valuable information, and a unique perspective on technology and the Internet.

The prospective subscriber now knows what to expect from this newsletter. It's stated simply and clearly. What's just as important is that Mr. Kleinman also knows exactly what he should be writing about in each issue. It's hard to overstate the importance of having a clearly defined purpose for your newsletter. If you vacillate between providing insights and information one week and pushing a product or service the next week, you'll quickly lose both credibility and the attention of your readers. Remember, the key to surviving your customers' inboxes is in finding a place in their minds where they will look forward to receiving your newsletter. If they are to look forward to it, they must feel secure in the knowledge of what the newsletter will contain. If you disappoint them, you'll lose that favored spot in their minds and they may not bother to read the next issue. And once they've missed reading one issue, it becomes very easy for them not to bother reading the next one, and so on.

You may need to fight to protect the editorial integrity of your newsletter. Even the most editorial and conversational newsletters can have some links in them, adding value to the experience by pointing out Web pages for the reader to visit. But if you have a terrific newsletter, someone in your organization may feel tempted to "monetize" it. Of course, it already has huge monetary value because it's building loyalty among your customers. But someone on high might want to see it become an immediate profit center, making a dollars-and-cents contribution to the quarter's balance sheet. At this point, it really is time to dig in your heels and fight.

How can you fight to keep your newsletter on track? It depends on your circumstances, but if you also do outbound email marketing, you can point out that the heavy promotional lifting is already being taken care of. There's no need to dilute the attraction of your newsletter by filling it with ads and special offers. You can also point to all the customer feedback emails that a decent newsletter will undoubtedly generate. Show the bosses that their customers really appreciate what your newsletter is giving them.

Give the Writer the Freedom to Create a Newsletter with Character.

For a newsletter to have a real personality, it needs to be written by one or two people who speak with one voice. Of all communications between your company and its audience, your newsletter is in the best position to deliver a sincere voice. This is particularly true if you succeed in the fight to keep out as much promotional content as possible.

For companies that have rigorous in-house guidelines on the style and content of all outbound communications, it can be a struggle to create a newsletter with true personality. But a brave management group and an inspired and gutsy writer can make it happen.

One example of a company that had the courage to hold its breath and see what happened is Bridges.com, the company mentioned in Chapter 10. The company describes itself in the usual, sober tone of a "proper" company:

> **North America's leading provider of career and educational planning solutions.**

That tone is fair enough for a corporate tag line. (Everyone has investors to please, one way or another.) But when it comes to the @*Bridges* newsletter, which is aimed at young adults, that voice changes dramatically.

Wayne, the alien career counselor, comes complete with the following disclaimer:

> **Disclaimer:** Do you realize that this freak is an alien? He has no training, lacks a decent sense of humour, and should probably be fired before he does any more damage. Take his advice at your own risk—our lawyers are worried that following Wayne's guidance may lead to mental instability and claims of alien abduction.

The style is decidedly out there, but the subscribers love it. Which is one of the reasons why Bridges.com Inc. really is "North America's leading provider of career and educational planning solutions." The company has done well by being prepared to stand out from the crowd with a unique, strong, and risky voice.

Interestingly, according to the man behind the voice, Jeremy Hiebert, he decided on an approach for the newsletter before the company even had an audience to talk to. He didn't pander to any particular demands or feedback; he decided on a voice that he liked. The response from his growing audience was overwhelmingly positive. Although they hadn't played any particular part in creating the voice, they enjoyed and respected the fact that it represented something different. People like a strong character online. In Jeremy's own words:

> We didn't have an audience when we started. We developed the site and content in a few weeks and then hoped for the best as they got sent out through Hotmail. I basically decided that I'd just write what came naturally and choose things that I found interesting. Bridges allowed me to do that, which was pretty cool.

I think so much of the writing on the web is designed to sell stuff, and make things sound glossier than they are. So I occasionally poke fun at the gloss.

A strong and definite character attracted the respect and attention of his readers.

Giving Your Newsletter a Voice Will Make Your Readers More Responsive.

In the cold world of cyberspace, it makes sense to jump at any opportunity to touch your customers in a way that is so personal that they'll write back to you. That's what you can achieve with a newsletter, but only if the writer's personality shines through.

Kevin Needham is the chief operating officer of MeMail.com, a company that delivers dozens of newsletters to over 426,000 readers around the world. After years of watching how readers respond to different types of newsletters, he has a pretty good feel for what works and what doesn't:

> We judged our best newsletters based on the number of responses we would get from the readers. The newsletters that got the greatest response were the ones that were written by an individual who shared his personality. We had other newsletters that were put together with off-the-shelf canned content that you buy from the news wires. But because they were written to such a general audience, these newsletters would give us the least response and feedback from our readers. By far the best newsletters we had, as far as response goes, were the ones that were written by individuals, with specific content. These were specialists within that particular area that were willing to share, and provide a feedback link so that their readers could interact with them.

That degree of responsiveness can make a huge difference in how your customers interact with your company. Web sites tend to be a one-way street, except for when people need help through your customer service functions. Promotional emails are pretty much one-way unless people make a purchase. And that kind of interaction is on a purely commercial level. So there is considerable value to be had from creating a more neutral, noncommercial channel of interaction through a newsletter. This way you can interact with your customers in a space that isn't fundamentally adversarial. You're not pushing them to make a purchase, and they're not fearful of a poor experience.

The most responsive of all the newsletters sent out by MeMail.com was *Mind & Body*:

MeMail.com: Mind & Body Digest

You and Food.

Dear Readers,

Thank you to the readers who've written in with very helpful comments on the Mind & Body Digest articles.

Here's a comment on last week's article (sensible weight loss) that got me thinking:

"Thanks for your reassuring article this week. What I have missed in your article is the importance of an emotional aspect of eating. One has to find out why one is eating. Only if that aspect is resolved, will the weight loss be permanent. Maybe you could find some articles that could help me and others in this respect?"

I did some online research and came up with surprisingly little (perhaps I was looking in the wrong places). I came across stacks of articles on the food-mood connection, but most of them were looking at the relationship in the opposite direction: at the impact of different types of food and eating habits on mood.

The author, Jackie Cooke, writes with a very easy, personal, and accessible style. It's little wonder that her readers were responsive. She writes as if the newsletter were a personal note between herself and each reader, one-to-one. The style looks easy to achieve, but it isn't. The easy way to write is how you were taught to write at school. Writing that is structured, objective, and formal may come easily to most people at college and in business, but a light style that is both casual and reassuring is very hard to achieve.

In fact, behind the light and easy style, Jackie takes a very structured and formal approach to building a newsletter that reads so easily. Here are some of her observations about her newsletter and how she puts it all together:

Articles usually contained a mixture of the following ingredients:

- information (usually the articles were based upon a published piece by a reliable and objective source),

- advice,

- motivation and inspiration,

- "big picture" commentary,

- hyperlinks to further relevant information, and

- readers' own (anonymous) words.

Some of the most positively received articles have been simple and contained only one clear message:

- Happiness,

- Posture,

- Smoking,

- Achieving a work-life balance,

- Shyness.

Other successful ingredients were:

- Clear, simple message,

- Conversational style,

- Personalization of message (e.g. "I was reading about xyz and started wondering how many of your readers..."),

- Invite reader input (the device worked excellently in compiling an article on how to improve quality of life, and in looking at how different people managed to give up smoking),

- Linkage to current event or issue,

- Respond directly to suggestions for articles that readers had written in with, and

- Provide a feedback email address that readers can write in to (this can be a good source of ideas for articles, although does take some time to work through and respond to—suggest autoresponder for acknowledging receipt of message).

Here's something else she says about her newsletter that gives you an insight into another vital ingredient of getting it right: caring about your subject and believing in it:

> While most people had signed up to this mailing list for reasons relating to personal health concerns, I feel very strongly about making the link between personal well-being with others' quality of life, shaped by issues of environmental sustainability, community well-being and awareness of the political choices implicit in our consumption decisions. In fact, it was the opportunity to deliver a "social responsibility" message that kept me enthusiastic about writing the articles from week to week.

If you don't care, if you don't have a passion for your subject, it's hard to maintain momentum, week after week. And it's that personal drive and vision of the author that is as important as the content when it comes to holding your subscribers' attention. Newsletters may be a great way to build a connection between readers and the author, but if the author's enthusiasm weakens, so will the connection.

Great Content Ensures That People Come Back for More.

In addition to writing with character and connecting with your audience in a personal way, you also need great content. Content is available free of charge by the truckload online. Gigabytes of content are produced every day. The Net is awash with words. The key is not just to pump out more and more of the same, tired information. You need to create content that offers genuine value to your readers. Great writing and great information.

Another of MeMail.com's top newsletters was *Media Beat*, written by Norman Solomon. The content of the newsletters comprised columns written by Mr. Solomon for other media. But the fact that the content was recycled didn't present a problem because the *Media Beat* newsletter made that content available to a whole new audience who would otherwise never have found it. And the key to the success of *Media Beat* lay in the quality of its writing and the information it provided.

In the introduction to a book written by Solomon in 1999, *The Habits of Highly Deceptive Media*, Jonathan Kozol wrote:

> The tradition of Upton Sinclair, Lincoln Steffens, and I.F. Stone does not get much attention these days in the mainstream press . . . but that tradition is alive and well in this collection of courageously irreverent columns on the media by Norman

Solomon. . . . He fights the good fight without fear of conse-
quence. He courts no favors. He writes responsibly and is metic-
ulous on details, but he does not choke on false civility.

It's little wonder his newsletter did so well. And when people write that well, it raises the bar for everyone who has
responsibility for writing a newsletter, either for themselves
or for their company. A newsletter, unfettered by the promotional imperative, is a place in which you can practice
great writing and share genuinely valuable information with
your readers.

The Challenges Facing Business Newsletters.

Even with the very best of intentions, if you're producing a
newsletter for your company, you're faced with a number
of significant obstacles, including the suspicious minds of
both your customers and your bosses.

At first, your customers may be suspicious of a newsletter that has a personal voice and is filled with great content,
because it's probably not what they are expecting. Consumers are quite rightly cautious about trusting messages
from companies, so it may take them a while to recognize
that your content-rich newsletter is not just another cun-
ning ploy designed to make them send you a check by the
end of the day. But if you keep at it, and if your readers
come to recognize your voice and appreciate the value of
the information you provide, those suspicions will slowly
be put aside. At that point, through having earned the trust
of your readers, you will have built an incredible asset for
your company.

Your bosses may be suspicious because it goes against
the grain to publish anything that is not promoting sales by
the end of the current quarter. Your newsletter will probably
come under the umbrella of the marketing department, in

one way or another, and be subject to its scrutiny. Is this in line with the current marketing plan? Does it support this month's promotions? Are you being a team player? This is the point at which you need to describe how the purpose of the newsletter is a long-term play, quite separate from short-term promotional considerations. The newsletter is written and designed to build trust. Trust will then work toward increasing sales. So you'll have to fight a little.

If you find that you're having to fight for the support of your superiors, show them the case of Jeremy Hiebert and @*Bridges*. That newsletter succeeded only with the support and steely nerve of senior management.

Some Tips on Presentation of the Content.

Should you use text or HTML for your newsletter? In large part that should be determined by the content you are providing. If there are strong visual elements, you may want to use HTML. But be cautious about turning your newsletter into a Web page that just happens to be delivered to someone's inbox. If it looks like a Web page, that's probably what it should be—if for no other reason than for its file size. Your readers won't thank you for hogging bandwidth while they're trying to download their email through a dial-up connection. Also, an HTML newsletter may make your readers a little more suspicious about your intentions. HTML is quite rightly associated with selling. So if your intention is that your newsletter be purely editorial in nature, don't run the risk of looking like you're out to make a sale. In addition, if your purpose is to create a personal voice that rings true, text is likely your best bet. Real people write using text, not HTML tags and photographs.

Whichever route you choose, use the first screen of each newsletter to give your readers a heads-up on the contents of that issue. First, show the title of the newsletter, so that people recognize who you are. Then you may want to follow the route taken by a lot of successful newsletters and provide a quick index of the contents of that issue. Here's how Quicken.ca opens its newsletters:

Quicken.ca Small Business Newsletter

June 1, 2001

Brought to you by Quicken.ca

Dedicated to your success

http://www.quicken.ca

This free newsletter appears every second Friday.

If you find it useful, please tell a friend or

family member about it.

IN THIS EDITION—June 1, 2001

• Use barter exchanges with care

• Internet trends and what you should do

• A guide to those weird ports on the back of your computer (Part 2)

• Ask a tax expert

• The Quicken.ca consultant

This introduction may lack in warmth and character, but Quicken uses a clean and clear opening that lets the reader know what's in store. Why does Quicken list the contents at the beginning? Because a computer screen doesn't afford the same scanning convenience as a sheet of paper. With a paper newsletter you can skim the whole thing in a few moments and zero in on the topics that interest you most. But online, while you're looking at the first few passages that fit on one screen, the rest of the contents are hidden. Your readers have no idea what's coming up. They don't know what to expect. It may be that some of your readers find you so compelling that they read every word, from beginning to end. But many of them will want to dip in and read a passage here and there, depending on what grabs their attention. By showing people a contents list on the first screen, you increase your chances of the newsletter being read, because you're letting everyone know what's coming up—and allowing people to jump forward to those parts that interest them the most.

Newsletters Hold Your Customers When Your Site Can't.

Your site may include great information about your products and services, but if a user is not about to make a purchase, of what value is that information? How much value does your site offer its visitors at those times when they are not interested in buying anything? Indeed, how much time do your customers actually spend at your site?

Newsletters fill the gap in between purchases and hold the attention of your customers. In fact, you'll likely find that a half-decent newsletter will become home to the most valuable content you have. The content on your site will generally be fairly static. Much of the text within your site needs to be clear, simple, and straightforward to make it easy for people to find their way around. But your newsletter isn't bound by such constraints. It's meant to be wordy. It's meant to change on a weekly or monthly basis. So if you do nothing else, encourage your site visitors to sign up for your newsletter. A decent newsletter will make your site look good even when it isn't being visited. The name and brand will grow through exposure in the newsletter.

If you find that your newsletter content has become so compelling that you can't stand the idea of anyone missing it, you can do what they did at NerdyBooks.com. They used the center space on their homepage as a spot to showcase some hot content from their newsletter. It's a great way to keep your homepage fresh and undoubtedly increases the number of site visitors who go on to sign up for the newsletter. On top of that, the newsletter content also brands the site with a unique voice that nobody can steal.

CHAPTER THIRTEEN

COPYWRITING ONLINE IS DIFFERENT

Aspects to Copywriting That Are Unique to the Web

It would be presumptuous to set out the "rules" for writing great copy online. There are no such rules. But here are some tips that should help online copywriters focus on some key differences when it comes to writing online.

Reek of Honest Humanity.

These words are taken from that great quotation from Ed McCabe that appears in Chapter 2 and is repeated here:

> To me, all advertising that is truly great reeks of honest humanity. Between every word you can smell the hot breath of the writer. Whether a result of wit, intelligence, insight or artfulness, great advertising invariably transmits itself to the receiver on a fragile human frequency.
>
> Source: *The Copywriter's Bible*, AD & AD Mastercraft Series.

The basic ingredient here is honesty. Honesty is fundamental to any copywriting, but particularly so online. Being honest is not about avoiding being caught on the wrong side of the truth. It's about the basic integrity of the intentions of the writer. Some copywriters might feel tempted to think along the lines of, "You know, I think I can persuade more people to buy this product if I add a little extra gloss to the message." When you do that, you cross over to the side of the weasel. Being a weasel means skirting the truth to make your story sound more convincing. Weasels leave out important facts and are dishonest by exclusion. Weasels tend to look down on their audiences and consider them to be of lesser intelligence. Weasels depend on fooling people. It's easy to become a weasel, and there may even be a short-term advantage. But as soon as you start thinking that way, you become cynical about marketing and cynical about copywriting. And cynics never write great copy.

If honesty is a basic ingredient of good writing, then to "reek of honest humanity" asks a great deal more. People are a lot smarter and more cautious about ads than they were a few years ago. They are more critical of what they read, see, and hear. The public, understandably, takes the position of considering companies as guilty of being weasels until they prove otherwise. In other words, the burden of proof is on the company and writer. To overcome a critical, cautious reader, your copy really does have to reek of honesty. It has to leave the reader in no doubt.

Reeking of honesty is one thing, but reeking of honest humanity is quite another. To reek of honest humanity, you have to put yourself into the copy you write. You have to put yourself and your own integrity on the line. You have to write from yourself, as an individual, directly to each member of your audience, one-to-one. Writing from yourself is quite different from writing from your company. When you write from your company, you make an internal shift, sliding responsibility for what you say from yourself to the corporation. It's a lot more comfortable that way. "Hey, it isn't me saying this—it's the company." If at this stage you are feeling that to "reek of honest humanity" is fanciful and unrealistic, you probably don't have what it takes to be a great online copywriter.

Ed McCabe wrote that line about copywriting in general, but it reads as if he wrote it specifically for the online experience. On the Net, people are a lot more sensitive to tone and subtext. By subtext I mean that while a company says one thing, it may mean the opposite. Here's a typical example of text from a Web site's contact link:

> Our Customer Service representatives will make every effort to respond to your email within 24 hours. However, if you haven't already done so, please check our Help section to see if your question is already addressed and answered.

The text says, in essence "We'll help you." But the subtext says, "You know, it's going to take us at least 24 hours to get back to you, so you might as well save us the bother and just check out our FAQ section." Text and subtext. Why are online customers more sensitive to subtext and tone than they are offline? Because ecommerce takes place in a common, shared space that was not created by the media or by corporations. It was created by millions of individuals who developed their own styles and cultures online and, at the same time, developed an uncommon sensitivity to tone and underlying meaning over the Net. You may be able to "'fool most of the people most of the time" offline, but you won't get away with it on the Web.

Online, Write in a Style That Recognizes the Distance between You and Your Reader.

To write successfully for the Web, you need to develop a different way of writing. Much of that difference is determined by the distance between you and the recipient.

If you're writing a brochure, you write copy that is printed on paper, folded, boxed, and then distributed to the end user—let's say an auto dealership. At some point the brochure is picked up and read by a prospective customer— maybe thousands of miles away from where you are and perhaps months after the words were first written. The distance between writer and reader could hardly be greater.

Online, you are much closer to the person who reads your text. The Internet is a place of immediate communication. You write your words on a computer monitor, and then they are read on a computer monitor by the prospective customer. There are no printers or delivery vans between you and your reader. And your copy may be read online within days or even hours of the time at which you wrote it. Short of meeting that person out on the street, this is about as close as you can get.

That proximity between you and the reader should prompt you to change the way you write. You should be writing in a way that is much closer to the way in which you talk and less like the way in which you write for print. It's your proximity that makes the difference. When you're writing online and can almost reach out and touch your customer, your writing should reflect that. You need to stop writing *at* them and change your tone. Write *with* them, almost as if you were talking with them. Loosen up. Relax your style.

Between the formality of the written word in print and the informality of speaking between friends, where should you find the right tone for writing online? That depends on the place and purpose of your text.

Imagine a line with print text on the far left and speech on the far right. In between those two extremes you will find different points on the line that will help you determine the correct writing approach for your Web site, for email, and for real-time live help. And in that order. Your style on the site will likely be a little more formal than for your emails. And your language on your emails will be a little more formal than in your live-help sessions. Those shifts in tone and approach depend on your proximity to your audience.

If You Want to Write Online, You Can't Look Down at People.

It's sometimes tempting to think that customers are stupid, that everyone who doesn't live in a big city is stupid, that people who just purchased their first computer are stupid, that people who have held the same job for the last 30 years are stupid. Most people have ways of looking down their noses at other people. And most of the time, that's OK, if you're comfortable feeling that way. But you can't get away with that kind of snobbery if you're writing online. You can't really afford to be like that if you write in the offline world, but you definitely won't get away with it on the Web.

Here's a quick story to test your own "other people are stupid" index. Perhaps this story is apocryphal—perhaps it's not:

> The story goes that a new computer owner called up Microsoft customer support with a question about the company's software. The customer service agent asked the customer to close all the windows and restart the computer. The customer then got up from his desk, walked around his apartment, closed all the windows and then returned to his computer and restarted it.

At this point it's tempting to howl with laughter and describe this customer as being too stupid to own a computer. But to do so is to become just another elitist snob in the world of high tech. For an older person who has never owned a computer before, or been around people who do, there was nothing stupid about following those instructions. New technology scares people. They don't know any of the terms that are so natural to long-time computer users. They don't know how computers work or what "windows" means in that context. They're not stupid; they're just new to computers.

Unfortunately, much of the way in which Web sites look and read has been arrived at by nouveau experts creating sites that are designed to impress their peers. These so-called experts may then become puzzled by the apparent stupidity of their audiences.

"Only a 2 percent conversion rate? We're losing 40 percent of our customers in the checkout area alone? Dammit —those customers must be stupid!" Not so. There are a number of reasons why conversion rates are low—and the way in which the copy is written is one of them. As a writer you have to try to cast off your own expertise and deep knowledge of the process and see everything through the eyes of someone who is completely unfamiliar with buying online. And for whom the "online experience" is just a tiny and very unimportant part of their life.

They need you to hold their hand, but not in a paternal way. They need you there as a friend who cares about them and wants to help them succeed in making the right purchase.

Recognize That You No Longer Own the Space in Which You Are Writing.

When you write a brochure, have it printed, and then have it distributed, you have an ownership of that mode of communication. It's your brochure, your space—and the way in which you write reflects that sense of ownership. When people pick up and read your brochure, they feel that tone of ownership in the message and largely accept it. It's your brochure and you can do what you like with it. But it doesn't work that way on the Web, because you no longer own the space in which you are writing. It's shared space, and those individuals whom you like to call your customers and prospects got there before you did. For this reason, your tone must defer to this fact. Your tone must recognize and respect the shared space and shared ownership. After all, once your prospects have spent a couple of hours on Usenet, Bizrate, and the like, they'll probably end up knowing more about your product or service than you do. It sounds unlikely, but it's true. Ask the sales assistants in a high street electronics store. Ask them about the level of knowledge of their customers today compared with the level five years ago. Ask them how many times a customer has come into the store and confounded them with superior knowledge of a particular product or manufacturer.

Online your audience members are connected, informed, and at ease in the space you're trying to sell in. You're on their turf. So the way in which you write has to reflect and respect that fact.

Be Aware of the Length of What You Write.

Readers don't read a screen the same way that they read words on paper. It's harder to read from a computer monitor, even large ones. It's tiring on the eyes. So if you are going to write longer copy, it had better be good and it had better be relevant. Many experts out there will say that copy should be very short because in the online environment people are in a hurry—surfing, browsing, moving from page to page and from site to site in search of the easiest way to achieve their intended goal. There's truth in that, but don't take it as gospel. Sometimes, when every expert says the same thing, it becomes an assumed truth, but that doesn't make it true all the time. Within the right context, and with a compelling message that engages the reader and gives her exactly what she wants to hear, text on a commerce site can go on for several screens.

However, if you are going to use long copy, here are some thoughts to keep in mind.

First, just because the copy is long doesn't mean that it has to *look* long. The appearance of length can be more threatening to the reader than the actual length. One easy way around this is to break your text up into small paragraphs. That way, 300 words broken into six paragraphs can look like a much easier read than 200 words in one, long paragraph. Given that people don't seem to like reading dense blocks of text online, it doesn't take much effort to lighten things up by writing in a style that makes more frequent use of the "Enter" key.

One vexing question that writers and usability engineers face is whether to keep a longer length of text on the one page, and hope that the reader keeps scrolling down, or to break the text up into one-screen sections with links from one screen to the next. If the lessons learned by direct marketers can be applied, and they probably can, you're better off asking your readers to scroll down that single page. The problem with single-screen sections that require the reader to click on a link to get to the next screen is that you'll never achieve anything approaching a 100 percent conversion rate. That is to say, with every new page, you'll lose a certain proportion of readers. The process of clicking and waiting for the next screen to download simply isn't seen as a reasonable trade-off for the pleasure of reading the next installment.

If you do decide to break up long lengths of text into screen-length sections and have a "Continue" button at the base of each, follow the direct-marketing rule from Chapter 8. That is to say, don't complete your thought or paragraph at the end of the page. When you break a compelling thought in half—between the first screen and the next—you'll increase the number of people who will click and wait for the next page to download.

Remember, the Hyperlink Is Not Always the Copywriter's Friend.

Many believe that the hyperlink, that clickable piece of underlined text, was invented by the man who gave us the World Wide Web, Tim Berners-Lee. Not so. In his book, *Weaving the Web*, Mr. Berners-Lee describes how the hyperlink came into being:

> Doug Engelbart, a researcher at Stanford University, demonstrated a collaborative workspace called NSL (oN Line System) in the 1960's. Doug's vision was for people to use hypertext as a tool for group work.

The hyperlink has been with us for a long time and has had a wonderfully liberating effect on the sharing and flow of information. As they say in *The Cluetrain Manifesto*, "Hyperlinks subvert hierarchy."

For the sharing and distribution of information, hyperlinks are great, but they are not always such a useful tool for copywriters trying to do their job at commercial sites. Part of the copywriter's craft is to carry the reader along a more or less predetermined path. A really good writer will be thoroughly engaging and entertaining as he weaves his tale and finally arrives at the point where he says, "Hey, you might want to buy this." But when a page is filled with hyperlinks, the visitor to a site is constantly distracted from the sales path.

Imagine a street vendor trying to sell vegetables to a group gathered around his stall while at the same time his stall is plastered with small signs saying things like, "If you like to cook, check out the skillets three stalls down." Or "Like fresh produce? Then you'll want to check out the fruit stall two aisles across." The information is great, and the visitors to the market will doubtless appreciate the directions. But these hyperlink equivalents make the vendor's job a great deal harder. While he's trying to sell his vegetables, his stall itself is undermining him by distracting the attention of his audience and encouraging them to go elsewhere.

The same happens on a retail site online. It's very hard to make a persuasive case to a visitor to make a purchase when that visitor is being distracted and often sidetracked by a host of hyperlinks that take people off the page. So be sure to confine hyperlinks to those places where they are actually needed. Don't undermine your own efforts to make the sale by giving your visitors multiple and overt opportunities to leave you halfway through the sale. Of course, if they want to leave, they can do that easily enough. But don't tempt them.

"Dead Fragments" Don't Engage Your Customers.

Many times there are conflicting opinions within the development group over the appropriate length of a piece of copy. The norm and the temptation is to reduce the length of copy as much as possible. Monitors are small, the attention of your audience is limited, and there are other things to go on the page. So the default position is to keep the text short. There are plenty of good reasons to do so, but you need to keep in mind that "dead fragments" won't engage your customers.

What is a dead fragment? It's what happens when you overedit. It's when you kill all emotion and remove the ability of a passage to connect with someone else on an emotional level. With apologies to Martin Luther King, Jr., here is a brief segment from his address from the steps of the Lincoln Memorial in 1963:

> I have a dream that my four children will one day live in a nation where they will not be judged by the color of their skin but by the content of their character.

Now cut that back to:

Have sons judged by character and not color.

What are you left with? A dead fragment. The core of meaning remains, but its soul and true message have been stripped away.

There are times when dead fragments work just fine, like when you want to add an instruction such as, "Click here to complete purchase." At that point, brevity is a virtue. But there are other times when a human touch can make all the difference. There are obvious places, such as in customer service communications, but also in less obvious places, such as within the text when you're describing your products.

When your copy loses a sense of humanity, or the feeling that it represents the voice of a real person, you are failing to understand or take advantage of the intensely personal nature of the Web.

Know That You Lose a Lot of Control over Appearance.

Traditional copywriters are used to keeping control over the appearance of text. Writers and art directors of printed materials control the appearance of their work in the knowledge that the layout and design they create will remain consistent between different newspapers and magazines. In fact, there used to be a third partner in the creative relationship in print—the typographer. Unfortunately that skill was almost completely destroyed by the advent of desktop publishing software packages that included dozens of different fonts and an equal number of ways in which to manipulate them. From the typographers' perspective, this advance spelled the near death of their craft. The appearance of text is no longer obsessed over in the way it used to be.

For those who mourn the passing of the typographer's skills, the Web can be a nightmare. Different monitor sizes, screen resolutions, browsers, and text-size settings will all confound your attempts to control the way that text appears on the screen. And if your site is being viewed on WebTV or a PDA, heaven help you. So more than ever, the power of what you write has to be carried by the meaning of the words themselves, and not their appearance.

How to Determine the Best Pace for Your Text.

Pace is a crucial element when it comes to holding the attention of your audience online. The pace of your text determines how quickly people will read what you have to say and how they feel about what you're saying:

You can increase pace like this. Short words. Short sentences.

Short paragraphs help too. Gets things moving! Really! The extra white space makes it look like an easy, fast read.

And the use of "and" at the beginning of a paragraph can speed things along as well. And for a brisk pace throughout, write how you speak. No grammar worries. Just like talking fast!

When you increase the pace like that, it tends to move the reader along more quickly. There's a kind of momentum being built that not only speeds things up, but also keeps the reader with you. The pace carries the reader along and makes it a little harder for him to stop.

However, that kind of approach won't always be appropriate. First, the language has to fit your own voice and the expectations of your audience. If you're an accountant with a Web site, a breathless, excitable tone to your text will likely send the wrong kind of message.

Second, the pace has to fit the purpose of that page within your site. If you're writing the product description text and want to tip your readers over into clicking that "Buy now" button, then a fast, excited tone can be just the ticket. However, if you're writing the privacy policy of your site, although the audience members are the same, their expectations within that context are not. They expect you to be serious and sincere when talking about privacy. They expect the pace to be slower. That said, there is no reason why privacy policies on sites have to be quite such a slow and hard read. If the lawyers have to write the bulk of it, then perhaps the copywriter could write a simple introduction that covers the main points in a way that is easy to read and easy to understand.

Third, you should vary the pace. Even if your site is selling racing snowboards or the latest bootleg CDs, you can't write at the same, excited pace throughout. It just doesn't feel right. It's not natural. Within all communications you should vary the speed and tone of what you say. If you keep the pace high-revving in first gear throughout, people will quickly sense that your voice doesn't sound genuine.

One way to get a feel for the pace that is right for the moment is to give it the "lean-forward, sit-back" test. The idea of "lean forward, sit back" comes from the different ways in which people sit at their computers and sit while watching TV. At their computers, people tend to lean forward, concentrating and interacting with whatever task they are involved with. When people watch TV, they tend to sit back, relaxed, not interacting and allowing their minds to slip into neutral. This difference in how people sit gives an interesting insight into a fundamental problem faced by those who have invested billions into bringing the world interactive TV. The big question being, do people really want to interact with their TVs? Or would they rather sit back and fall asleep?

In any event, when people are working their way around your site, they are not always in the exact same lean-forward mode. There are variations. While surfing through your site, seeing what you have to offer without any immediate intention of signing up or making a purchase, people may not be as "lean forward" as they are when they get down to the moment before hitting that "Submit" button. The degree of concentration and interaction varies according to the task at hand.

As a rule of thumb, consider keeping the pace of your copy at a moderate level when the readers are in more of a sit-back mode—such as when reading an introduction to your company or a description of your customer service policies. But increase the pace when the readers are interacting, intent on completing a task and leaning forward. Write at a faster pace the more they lean forward, and at a slower pace as they relax and sit back. Is this a hard and fast rule? No. But a picture in your mind of the body position of your prospect or customer is certainly one good indicator of how you should pace your copy.

A Loud Voice Is the Refuge of the Weak.

The skill of writing at a pace that is appropriate to the moment is one that has been learned and mastered by dozens of writers offline, long before the Web came along. It's an old skill. However, there is an aspect of pace that you have to be careful about when writing online. And that is the volume of your voice.

Offline, when writing direct mail, a radio script, or even a print advertisement, the culture allows you to raise your voice as much as you like. That is to say, when people listen to a radio spot that goes on and on about Bob's great deal on used cars, they expect hyperbole. They both expect and accept Bob's ludicrous rant. And that's OK. It doesn't trouble them because it fits within the culture of radio ads. It's what they expect from Bob, and they simply adjust their own personal volume dial and accord the message the attention they feel it deserves. They have been listening to and filtering radio ads for decades and know how to handle them.

Online, there is no such acceptance of advertising overstatement. So while you increase the pace of your text in an outbound email, you have to consider the "loudness" of your voice, because the readers won't do it for you. If you do exceed the boundaries of what the readers will accept, they will likely conclude that your email belongs with all those other loud messages they receive each day—the spam that ends up in the trash.

In short, don't shout. Hyperbole doesn't fit well within the still evolving culture of commerce online. People are still learning and adjusting. They're still feeling their way forward when it comes to handling marketing online. They can handle Bob's brash tones offline, with no ill effects to themselves or Bob. But they can't and won't do so online.

That said, the very best copy in any environment avoids raising your voice too much. As copywriter Neil French says:

> What have I learned over the years? That instinct discounts superlatives. That adjectives stretch credulity. That blatancy does not command respect. That overstatement creates resistance. And that inside every fat ad there's a thinner and better one trying to get out. In short, the less said the better.
>
> Source: *The Copywriter's Bible*, AD & AD Mastercraft Series.

Don't Rewrite Those Navigation Links.

There is one area in which even the most enthusiastic writer should be discouraged from showing too much imagination. That is in the area of writing those familiar text links that are found on most sites. For instance, when people go to a site and look for more information about the company, they look for the "About Us" link. "About Us" is the term used on most sites, and Web users have come to expect those words. People scan for them and recognize their shape on the screen even before they read the words themselves. As a result, it makes very little sense to try writing funky variations on the theme. An inexperienced writer may suggest "Our Company" or "Company Info" as alternative text. But why do that? Those aren't the words your visitors will be looking for. You're simply creating questions in their minds. "Hmm. I wonder if this is where I'll find the 'About Us' information?"

In the area of simple navigation links, it makes sense to do what everyone else is doing and avoid being different or imaginative. There are plenty of other places from which to project the site's unique personality.

What People Read and What They Don't Read on Retail Sites.

When people come to a retail site online, they are either curious about what you sell or already have a pretty clear idea about what they want to buy. People also tend to be fairly purposeful when they arrive at your site. In a bricks-and-mortar mall, people may have time on their hands and wander in and out of stores with no immediate purpose or direction. This doesn't appear to be the case online. Finding the Web site they want and enduring the purchase process online is hard enough as it is. As a result, people are looking for information that helps them achieve their goals more easily.

What kind of text helps people achieve their purpose?

- Clear directions that tell them how to achieve their goal.

- Comprehensive product or service descriptions that give users enough information to make them feel comfortable making the purchase.

- Simple, brief and sincere copy that reassures the buyer that the site can be trusted.

What kind of copy is ignored?

- Long privacy policies and user agreements.

- Instructions on how to use or navigate the site.

- Long FAQ pages.

- Long text on shipping and return policies.

- Any block of text that is self-serving without offering necessary information or a benefit to the reader—as in, "Here at JohnSmith.com we are at the forefront of widget innovation, blah, blah, blah."

With this in mind, you might want to go through your site and think about removing all those copy elements that people don't read and see how that might impact your sales. Also, do some server log analysis and see how many people click through to your FAQ page, your privacy policy page, and your shipping and returns policy page. And see how long people stay on those pages. Are they staying long enough to read more than a couple of words? The chances are that very few people are.

So what are the implications for the conversion rates on your site? What if you cut all those pages out? You may find some key information that users need to know, but isn't being found or read. In that case, remove that information from those "dead" pages and place it on the pages where you know the user will read it. And keep it brief.

Assumptions of Privacy and Decency.

Once you realize almost nobody is reading your privacy policy, it's time to pause and think. If nobody is reading the policy, you can put anything you like in there. You can say you'll sell everyone's personal information to anyone who cares to buy it. Bury that line deep within page 6 of the policy and you're almost guaranteed that nobody will ever read it. The same goes for your shipping and returns policy. You can say that customers are fully liable for return shipping costs, plus a restocking fee, and nobody will be any the wiser.

The trouble is, when you do this—and plenty of sites do —you're undermining the basis of any kind of lasting relationship between your company and its customers. Visitors to your site arrive with an assumption of privacy. They assume that their personal information will be safe in your hands—unless you very clearly state otherwise on a key page that everyone will read.

Knowledge of who reads what on which pages at your site brings with it some responsibilities. First, you need to know where the dead spaces are, so that you can be sure they're not impacting on your conversion rates. Second, you need to think about how other information in those dead spaces might undermine your long-term relationships with your customers.

CHAPTER FOURTEEN

THE HEART OF A GREAT COPYWRITER

Offline Copywriting Lessons That Still Apply Online

The tips and thoughts in this chapter differ slightly from those in the last because they can be applied to any medium. These are thoughts that any experienced copywriter will recognize. They belong in this book because so many people have been shanghaied into being online copywriters without any training or background in the craft.

Listen Long and Hard before You Write.

Marketers are not used to listening. They are used to researching through polls, surveys, and focus groups. They are used to buying information on demographics and psychographics. But that's not the same as listening. When you use research, you control the process. You ask the questions you want answered and anticipate the answers you will receive. Ultimately, it's a narrow process confined by the imagination and intentions of the researchers themselves. Listening is a very different process, a very different skill, and it brings with it some very different demands. In a shared environment like the Internet, those who don't listen are quickly identified and ignored. Companies that don't listen are seen as "not getting it," and their brand equity declines.

For the copywriter online, the opportunity and willingness to listen is a core skill. Why? Because you have no hope of engaging your customers in any meaningful way if you don't know who they are or what they want. It's like going on a blind date and keeping your eyes closed and your fingers in your ears. If you can't see or hear the person or people to whom you are talking, it's impossible to move forward. You will be as ignorant during your tenth encounter as you were during your first.

Copywriters offline work with very limited sight and hearing, provided by the research that lands on their desks and whatever other research they undertake themselves. But copywriters online have incredible opportunities to listen.

Listening online can be achieved in a variety of ways.

- You can listen by building and saving profiles of visitors and buyers. At the very least a copywriter should ask to see the aggregated behaviors of site visitors. A smart copywriter will also study individual profiles and try to build a picture of individual customers. It's the individuals you need to hold and picture in your mind as you begin to write, whether you're writing a homepage, the last screen of the purchasing process, or an email.

- You can listen by adding feedback opportunities throughout the site. These can be custom-built feedback buttons that link to quick surveys that collect customer reactions and comments. Or you can use an

outside supplier like OpinionLab.com, which gives
you a ready-made feedback system, including access
to detailed reports on the feedback you receive. Either
way, aggregated and individual feedback should
always be distributed to the copywriters.

- You can build onsite discussion areas. Dell helps its
customers find solutions to their problems through its
DellTalk Forums. These forums are there as a means
for consumers to share their knowledge of the Dell
computers and to help each other with problems. It's
a great customer service tool, as the total combined
knowledge of all the participating computer owners
certainly exceeds the product knowledge of any individual Dell customer service representative.

But these discussion areas are also great places for Dell
copywriters (and copywriters from competing companies)
to listen. By reading the posts of your customers, on a
regular, obsessive basis, you learn a number of things.
You learn about what really interests your customers.
You find out what they worry about, what they are looking for, what they're angry about. A day spent reading a
discussion area will teach you more about the audience
to which you are writing than a dozen research reports.

In addition, you'll also get a feel for the language the
customers use, the way they write, and the level at which
they communicate and share. Should a copywriter then
plan on simply emulating the language and tone of the
discussion participants when he or she next writes an
email campaign? No, that makes about as much sense
as the father who starts talking like a 17-year-old in the
faint hope that it will bring him closer to his teenage
son. It doesn't work like that. But the more you listen,
the better you'll be able to match your company's voice
to the needs and sensibilities of your audience.

Some would suggest that matching your voice in response to the sensibilities of an audience is inherently dishonest. If you keep changing your voice, how can any one of them truly be yours? It's not dishonest at all, or it needn't be. People constantly adjust their voices to different audiences and circumstances. You don't speak in the exact same way to your colleagues as you do to your children or to your in-laws. Your core nature and beliefs can remain unchanged at the same time as your voice shifts to match the circumstances.

- You can also listen in on outside discussion areas. Topica, a service that hosts email discussion lists and newsletters, published a study in January 2001 in which Topica profiled the experiences of one company, Lawson Software. Here is an excerpt from that study:

At a Lawson User Conference in April '99, an attendee distributed fliers about an HR software email list he had created at Topica. Many subscribed and were interested to learn that these lists were free and easy to set up and use.

Shortly thereafter, Lawson users created two more lists that were instantly promoted on the original list. One was for Lawson System Administrators, which grew to 300 subscribers in the first week of its existence. That list has nearly tripled to almost 800 subscribers today. The other list, which now has 600 subscribers, was created to discuss Lawson's financial software solutions.

This created a trend within the Lawson user community to set up discussion lists around many of Lawson's software packages.

Naturally, Lawson was more than happy to see its customers gathering together in this way. There's a huge amount for everyone to learn by listening in. Once again, the first of those to log in and listen to what Lawson customers are talking about should be the Lawson copywriters.

- Listen by camping out in the customer service area. Perhaps the best way to understand your audience is to be a fly on the wall in the customer service area. Listen in on live calls coming into the call center. Hear what customers say and what the customer service agents say in reply. Some agents are great, and you can learn a lot from the language and tone they use. Some agents are poor, and you can learn from them also. Do the same with the live-chat agents who type instant replies to customer inquiries on the site. When you look over these people's shoulders, you are watching a live performance of your site. It's real and it's happening now. You can see where and why people stumble, where they become confused, why they can find some places on the site and not others. You can hear their frustrations and begin to recognize their voices. It's a foolish company that keeps its front-line staff in isolation and lets all that knowledge remain buried in some knowledge base somewhere. This is the information every copywriter online needs to stay current with. Imagine the advantage this gives you compared with offline copywriters in their near blind and deaf condition.

- Listen by getting copied on inbound customer emails. If you work for a very large company, you won't want every customer email in your inbox when you get to work each morning. But read as many as you can, consistently, day after day. People are incredibly up-front and frank in their emails. Sometimes they are rude and use bad language. But for a copywriter, it's all great stuff—you're tapping into the unvarnished feelings of your audience. Short of conducting your business in a concert hall, with your customers seated right there in front of you, this is as immediate and as connected as business can get.

Always Take the Side of Your Customers.

This is about the attitude you bring to your writing. It's about whose side you're on. Are you on the side of your company, in pursuit of maximum sales? Or are you on the side of the customers, helping them to get exactly what they really want or need at a good price and with great service?

At first glance, it might appear that the only truly honest answer is the first one. It's the company that pays your salary, and you should be on its side. But there's an apparent conflict here, because to write great copy, you really need to be on the side of your customers. You need to have a place where you sit inside their heads and get a genuine feel for how they react to your site, how they feel about what you are offering—and what it would take to make them feel more comfortable about making a purchase.

Pushing sales, oblivious to how the people who make up your audience feel, will take you only so far. On those occasions when pushing hard results in a sale, all you're left with is a customer with buyer's remorse and a lot of bad feelings about your company. If you really want to serve your company's best interests, take the customers' side. That results in a win for everyone. And as a copywriter, you get to learn more and more about how other people feel. It's a rare gift to be able to understand those feelings and an incredible asset when applied to the craft of copywriting.

Stephen Covey, in his book *The 7 Habits of Highly Effective People*, talks about "empathetic listening":

> When I say empathetic listening, I mean listening with intent to understand. I mean *seeking first* to understand, to really understand. It's an entirely different paradigm.
>
> Empathetic (from *empathy*) listening gets inside another person's frame of reference. You look out through it, you see the world the way they see the world, you understand their paradigm, you understand how they feel.

When you write to your audience and they recognize you through what you say and how you say it, that's a powerful thing. When they know and sense that you really do have their best interests at heart, that you're empathetic, they'll trust you more and they'll buy more. And once the purchase is made, they'll feel happy about it afterward.

It's just a matter of shifting attitudes. Instead of trying to push your products, serve your customers. As soon as you're on their side, you'll start selling more.

Know What to Say before You Worry about How to Say It.

As with any craft, copywriters can be vain and driven by ego more than by common sense. When this happens, they pay too much attention to *how* they say something, rather than spending most of their time determining *what* to say.

Here's an example. If you sign up for the email updates at the Southwest Airlines site, Southwest will send you what it calls:

Southwest Airlines' Click 'n Save® E-mail

Updates—the simplest way to stay informed of Southwest Airlines sales and promotions

Sounds like a great idea. But if you sign up, the first email confirmation you receive reads as follows:

NO ACTION REQUIRED

Thank you for your interest in the Southwest Airlines Internet Specials Mailing List.

And it continues in the same vein for a while. What is significant here is not that the writing is wooden and lifeless, but that it is saying absolutely the wrong things. First, you don't want to welcome someone to the most interactive business environment ever conceived with the words "NO ACTION REQUIRED." It's like having a sign hanging over the entrance to a neighborhood bar that reads "No talking allowed." What's the point of going out for a drink if you can't talk? And what's the point of doing business on the Web if you can't interact?

Second, when he or she says, "Thank you for your interest in the Southwest Airlines Internet Specials Mailing List," the writer is still getting it wrong. Those prospective customers have absolutely no interest in the list itself. It's not the list that excites them. It's the promise they read on the site— "stay informed of Southwest Airlines sales and promotions." It's the deals that are interesting, not the mailing list.

Beyond the carelessness of the text is a deeper problem. A huge opportunity has been lost. This is the first point of personal contact between Southwest Airlines and the recipient of this first email. That moment should be treated as golden. You have just a few moments to capture the reader's attention and a very small corner of her heart. This is the moment when you try to make a genuine, human connection that makes your reader feel positive, warm and comfortable about your email. "NO ACTION REQUIRED" doesn't get that job done.

This is an obvious and important example. But you need to pay attention to the "what" of what you say at every point. There are no prizes for saying the wrong thing beautifully.

Know Your Company Better Than Anyone Else.

A copywriter in the offline world who is faced with writing an ad for a chair manufacturer, for example, has a tough but relatively straightforward job. He has to research the chairs and the company. He has to understand the media choice in which the ad will run and the people who read those magazines and newspapers. He has to understand and write to the strategy laid out by the manufacturer and, if he works in an ad agency, by his colleagues in research, media, and account management. He has to work closely with a designer. Is it easy to produce great copy offline? No. Most ads are horrible, the rest are indifferent, and a statistically insignificant number are fabulous. That's where you want to be. You want to reside in the glow of statistical insignificance. To get there, the writer of a print ad has to think long and hard to produce great work.

Now consider the job facing a copywriter with broad responsibilities at a Web site. A Web site is not an ad, nor is it a brochure. Any one screen is not an isolated communication or expression. Every screen is connected with every other screen, directly or indirectly. That page from which you are trying to sell a chair may also contain links to window coverings, to customer service, plus an invitation to subscribe, sign up, buy, or comment. It may also contain links that take the reader off the site entirely. It's not an ad placed on a magazine page in splendid isolation. It's a single screen within an entire company's "space" online. That makes writing a great deal more complicated. It means that each page you write has to be written within a much broader context. It also means that a much larger number of people will be watching and influencing which words go on that screen.

One result of this very complex scenario that faces the online writer is that he has to know the company and its products better than anyone else. He has to know how each page fits within the bigger picture, how each product fits within the broader merchandising strategy, how each email impacts the longer-term marketing plan, how each extra line written or removed impacts on the user experience.

Knowing your company and its site thoroughly is as important as understanding your audience intimately. You have to be the master of both. This is a challenge at the best of times, but impossible if writers are not given sufficient authority and accorded sufficient respect to achieve these goals. Copywriters need access to meetings and planning sessions that may not be directly related to the writing of copy. They need access to reports and research findings and, as mentioned earlier, access to all those front-line staff who interact with customers on a day-to-day basis.

Even the Short Text Deserves Attention.

There's a temptation to write short text in a hurry. But before you rush those words too quickly, there are two points to consider here. First, short text is sometimes the most important text. It may be the copy used as the "short description" of a product or service being sold from your site. Perhaps it's only 10 or 20 words. And if you have hundreds or even thousands of products on your site, it's tempting to have a junior writer or intern write those short descriptions. But the quality of those few words can have a dramatic impact on conversion rates.

Ask the people involved with the creation of catalogs or direct-mail packages about the short pieces of text used to describe products or used as captions to photographs, and they will tell you that those few lines can make a big difference. It makes sense to pay the same close attention to short text on your site. After all, if most people are just skimming your pages, it's the short text that will catch their attention and ultimately hold or lose their interest.

The second reason why you should pay closer attention to short text on your site is that writing these pieces well can go a long way toward turning a casual browser into a customer. Short text, when done right, gives you the hook to hold attention and drive interest.

To illustrate the point, here is an exercise in writing a short caption for a photograph. Imagine you're writing an advertisement to promote a golfing magazine. The ad shows images of various pages from upcoming issues of the magazine. Each image has a short caption. Why bother with captions? Because they are some of the most widely read snippets of text in any publication. Which parts do you read first when leafing through a magazine? If you're like most people, you read the photo captions first. So in the offline world, captions get lots of attention from a good copywriter.

Now imagine this image shows a photograph of Jack Nicklaus teeing off, with an excited crowd in the background. What should you say? Here's a first stab:

Jack Nicklaus tees off in front of an expectant crowd.

A lot of writers would leave it at that. Job done. But it's a very poor caption so far. All it does is describe what's in the photograph. And what's the point of that? It's a wasted opportunity. There's no point in using text to try to describe what is already plain to see. Here's a second attempt:

Jack Nicklaus, six times Masters winner, at the 11th hole of the Augusta National in Georgia.

This one is better because it adds information that the image itself doesn't provide. Now you know where he is and a key fact about his track record. The image and the picture are working together. But given that the purpose of the brochure is to sell subscriptions to the golfing magazine, is this caption working hard enough yet? Not really. Here's a third try:

In the next issue—three hot tips from Jack Nicklaus, the perfectionist who used to hit 300 practice shots a day at the age of 10!

Now you have a caption that is a little longer, but is working much harder to sell the magazine. It's pushing for fast action because of the upcoming feature of Nicklaus in the very next issue. It's promising a "deliverable"—those three hot tips. And it's engaging our interest on a personal level. Did you know that Nicklaus hit 300 practice balls a day when he was 10? Can you imagine your kids doing that? Do you wonder what kind of childhood he had while he was obsessing over golf?

A caption, or any short length of text, tends to capture a reader's attention first. It's the low-hanging fruit, the easiest and fastest text to digest.

The Jack Nicklaus caption could have gone through several more revisions and improvements. But here are some questions for development groups online. How much time and attention is focused on the short text on your site? Does someone write and rewrite those words, time and again, in search of maximum impact? Is every link, every product description, every subhead and heading, given this kind of close-up attention? If it isn't, it should be. Whether on your site, in your emails, or in a newsletter, it's the short text that will likely impact your conversion rates the most.

Here's some short text from the Sun & Bodycare page at the Lancôme Paris Web site:

> Lancôme believes that sun and body care should be an experience of general well-being, where the sensuality of texture and pleasure of a delicate fragrance form a beauty ritual which stays with women throughout the day, releasing their mind while caring for their body.

First, 44 words is far too long for just about any sentence, especially on an ecommerce site. In this particular spot the text covers a huge range of thoughts and emotions. It's about the experience of well-being, and the sensuality of texture, and the pleasure of a delicate fragrance, and beauty rituals, and releasing one's mind, and caring for one's body. But one purpose this text does not appear to have is to drive the user forward toward making a purchase. This kind of potpourri of fanciful thoughts does a great job of creating a vague wallpaper of feel-good sensations. It works for beauty product packaging and countertop materials, but it doesn't do the job online. In a small space like this, job one is to move the user forward with a positive attitude. Yes, paint a brief feel-good picture, but keep it short and add in the words necessary to move the user along the sales path.

Delight People by Paying Extra Attention Where It's Least Expected.

At the top of some steps that lead down to one of the beaches at Monterey, California, a sign says:

> So that others may enjoy our fragile tidepools and kelp forests, please take only photographs, leave only footprints.

What an unexpected and pleasant surprise. That sign could so easily have read, "Take nothing and leave nothing." Same message, but no heart. The writer not only had the talent to craft a much more engaging message, but also took the time to do so. Which brings us to another important attribute of any great writer online: You need to give a damn. If not, that lack of heart will find subtle expression in every word you write.

Here's another example of writing with character, where character is usually absent. Lester Moore was a Wells, Fargo Co. station agent in the cowboy days of the 1880s. He's buried in the famous Boot Hill Cemetery in Tombstone, Arizona. Here's what it says on his headstone:

Here lies Lester Moore
Four slugs from a .44
No Les No More.

And here you can see where the management of a New York Crunch gym thought a little beyond the traditional "Authorized Personnel Only" sign:

Staff Only.
Don't feel left out.
Please apply at the
front desk.

What a great way to turn a negative message into a recruitment opportunity. Neat writing like this takes place when copywriters take genuine pleasure in their craft.

Show a Little Enthusiasm.

Genuine enthusiasm is a wonderful, uplifting, and contagious condition. Whatever they're talking about, enthusiastic people usually make those around them feel good. They make them smile.

Enthusiasm is also an important component of communication online, through your site and your emails. And while personal enthusiasm may not be very acceptable within offline business communications, it fits in just fine on the Web. The Motley Fool site at Fool.com is enthusiastic, as are its emails and even its books. The @*Bridges* newsletter about career counseling for young adults is enthusiastic. And so is the site that sells the Fish! Philosophy of employee motivation and learning.

At FishPhilosophy.com they're selling a variety of packages, including a book, videos, and seminars that are all aimed at companies hoping to motivate their employees to achieve more and get more enjoyment from their work. The Fish! site could easily have been just another bland, company services site with the same old look and the same old text. But it's not like that. It looks, reads, and feels like the promise of its own philosophy. It looks like fun.

To get that feeling behind your site, the designers and the writers have to get charged up and really feel good about what they're creating. When you're creating something online, you have to feel enthusiastic and that feeling has to be genuine.

When that happens, when you really feel good about what you're writing, everything changes. You no longer write according to the skills you've learned at some academic level. The "skill" of writing is no longer a visible part of the process; it just hums away in the background. Instead, when you feel good about what you're saying, the words just flow out of your fingertips. That kind of energy in copy is invaluable. It captures and holds the readers' attention. It makes them want to stay close, keep reading, and find out what's behind that good feeling.

Of course, it also has to be genuine. You can't fake it. So here's the question—if the subject of the site is not inherently fun or exciting, how can one be genuinely excited about it? Well, that's part of the copywriter's skill. You have to find something within what the company has to say that intersects with what your audience really wants to hear. You have to find something to say that really is good news to the ears of both the company and the customer. When you've found that nugget, then you can sit back and say, "Hey, I really do believe in this. I can get excited about this. This is honest, it's right, and I feel good." That's the point at which you can build up some real enthusiasm about what you're writing. And when that enthusiasm becomes apparent in the text that appears on your site or in your emails, you'll do a much better job of engaging the attention and interest of your readers.

Keep It Simple.

Keeping things simple is excellent advice for any writer in any medium. Here are a few great examples of how simple writing works best. These are taken from *Editing and Design* by Harold Evans. The first line is the unnecessarily long version; the second is the simple version:

- The theatre has seating accommodation for 600.
- The theatre seats 600.

- They enjoyed recreational activity.
- They liked games.

- Warmer conditions will prevail.
- It will be warmer.

- The teacher supply situation is serious.
- Teachers are scarce.

Harold Evans wrote his book to help journalists learn the skills of their trade. But he could just as well have written it for people with aspirations to write for the Web. The Web calls out for simple language built on short words. That kind of language is very close to the natural style of the spoken word and fits in very well with how people like to communicate online.

The challenge here is that it is much harder to write simply. When you write without paying enough attention, you'll probably use two or three times the number of words you need. But if you sit down and think very carefully about what it is you're really trying to say, you'll realize that there is a great deal of fluff that can be cut out. It takes more time, but results in much greater clarity and a much easier read for your customers.

Know What You're Saying—and Write More Than One Draft.

It may sound old-fashioned, but great writing is rarely achieved in the first draft that you write. Online there is this temptation to write quickly. Everything has to be done on "Internet time." Unfortunately, fast writing is rarely good writing. This is the case whether you are writing a long, conversational newsletter or a short, tight headline or product description.

In the case of the headline, which is often the shortest of all texts, multiple drafts are a necessity. And you need time as well. You need time to write out a few drafts and let them sit. Leave them overnight and come back to them with a fresh perspective. And always keep referring to the briefing document. Within that brief you should be able to find the sentence or paragraph that encapsulates the purpose and message of the headline. If you have no brief or it has been poorly written, you'll have to do this stage for yourself. But be sure that you have that statement of purpose clearly in mind as you write. This is your guide to telling you *what* to say. It can help if you go as far as writing that statement on a slip of paper and taping it on the top of your monitor.

A clear statement about what your headline should be achieving helps you avoid the mind games that copywriters can fall victim to. Let's say that you come up with a truly wonderful, insightful, and witty headline. It's the best you've ever written. You might be tempted to go with it, because it sounds so great and makes you look so smart for having written it. But the more you like the line you penned, the more important it is to raise your eyes a few inches to that slip of paper. Because if the headline is not 100 percent on brief, then it's the wrong line, however sweet it may sound.

For the same reason, it's important to approach any online writing task in the knowledge that you'll be writing a second and maybe third and fourth draft. It's important for short text, because it's so easy to get off track. And it's important for longer text, like newsletters, because those more conversational passages can become a little too loose and flabby. So once you've written that first draft, don't click the "Send" button. Create a little emotional distance between yourself and what you've written. It's hard to let a headline or paragraph go when you've just given birth to it. So walk away for a few hours. When you come back you will be able to look at what you've written from a much more objective viewpoint. For the same reason, you may want to put your ego on the back burner and pass what you've written around to some colleagues or friends. Every writer is defensive to some degree, so it's important to develop work habits that give you the opportunity to take a second look at what you've written and redraft it. You get the prize for getting it right, regardless of how many drafts that may take.

CHAPTER FIFTEEN

10 EASY WINS WITH STRONG COPY

The First Places to Improve the Impact of Your Copy

Author Douglas Adams, of *The Hitchhikers Guide to the Galaxy* fame, once said:

> Human beings, who are almost unique in having the ability to learn from the experience of others, are also remarkable for their apparent disinclination to do so.

How true. With that in mind, it's safe to assume that copywriters will not become the leading stars of the online firmament in the very near future. In the meantime, there are some first steps you can take that will increase conversion rates at your site and make your visitors more inclined to come back and spend their money with you again. These are the easy wins, the things you can try first in the hope that everyone else in the organization will see what you're achieving and accord great copy the attention and respect it deserves. You'll recognize some of the subjects of these steps from previous chapters. They are put together here to give you a quick overview and action plan that you can start applying as soon as you'd like.

Step 1

Make that first email connection as personal and as compelling as possible.

If you work hard enough and get enough things right, a prospective customer will take an action that says, "Speak to me." This is a moment like no other. Hundreds of visitors may come and go before one will pause, type in her email address, and say, "I want something from you." Perhaps that person emailed you with a specific request for information regarding a product or service. Perhaps she opted in to some email promotions you send out. Perhaps she wanted to receive your monthly or weekly newsletter. But whatever the purpose of this first point of contact, it should cause a "first customer contact" alarm to go off in your office.

Here's your checklist of what to do in response to that moment.

- Try to avoid autoresponders. If this is the first time a customer has contacted you, you need to get back to that person with a message that is clearly personal. "Personalization" is not enough, however sophisticated the software. The words need to be *personal*. If each message can't be written one at a time, then at least the prepared text should be written with care.

- Know what to say. When a visitor reaches you through your site, be very aware of what she is looking for and expecting. If she signs up for emails about remodeling kitchens, don't send her a reply that starts by saying,

"Thank you for your interest in our home improvement email program!" She has no interest in your home improvement email program. She's interested in making her kitchen a place she can really enjoy. Knowing what to say is the first thing you need to get right. In doing so, you will put yourself way ahead of the pack. Most emails never get past first base, because they start out by saying something that fails to connect with the reader's true interest.

- Know how to say it. Saying the right thing may be the most important first step, but saying it in the right way makes a big difference also. The tone and character of the first message you send back, that welcome email, will determine how that customer feels about you and your company. Is the tone of the email too stiff and formal? Is it overly promotional? Is it too warm and syrupy? Whatever tone you deliver through that first contact, that's the first impression you'll create, and that's how your company will be judged in the customer's mind.

It's hard to overemphasize the importance of that first moment of personal contact with your customers. They may have formed a preliminary impression from your site, but the impression that will direct their feelings about your company to a far greater extent is determined by the way in which you interact with them one-on-one.

The messages within emails, particularly those that go out early in your relationships with your customers, probably aren't getting the right level of attention right now. In fact, you may find that the text being used was first written months or even years ago and hasn't been thought about since. There's a great opportunity to improve both conversion rates and customer loyalty by going back to these emails and making them work harder.

Step 2

Add some zip and clarity to your short text.

Here's an area that you can start work on right away. Short text appears in numerous places on your site, in your emails, and in your newsletters. This is the text that is usually written quickly and without a great deal of thought. It may be the brief instructional text that tells someone what to do next on your site, or a product description, or the link descriptions in a newsletter. But wherever you find short text online, there's almost always a way in which you can improve it.

Instructional text on your site should be reviewed for brevity and clarity. Users generally don't read long blocks of instructional text, so if you have a very important point buried in paragraph five, it probably won't be read. Try to abbreviate what needs to be said; and if there is background information that a few users might want to read, create a link through to it on another page, rather than forcing every user to confront an overly long block of directions. Also, watch for clarity, because developers will sometimes make assumptions about the level of online experience of their users. Don't assume knowledge that your visitors may not have.

Step 3

Include a call to action.

Many sites appear shy to actually ask for the sale. Product descriptions sit there, passive and waiting for the visitors to take the plunge, or not. Email-address sign-up boxes for newsletters appear alone, with no words to encourage people to sign up now. Homepages rest on their laurels, showcasing the site contents, but making no effort to drive people deeper into the site. Promotional emails capture a reader's attention and then let it go before any action is taken.

Your site and your business depend on actions being taken on your site and through your emails. You need to identify each and every action point and ensure that the accompanying text is attempting to close that action there and then.

Here's a typical example of the text that accompanies the newsletter sign-up form on a homepage:

Sign up for our newsletter:

```
[                  ]
```

Your email address

And here's how the same opportunity is handled by Dr. Ralph Wilson on his "Doctor Ebiz" homepage:

> You can **receive FREE OF CHARGE** two of Dr. Wilson's $12 eBooks, **Demystifying Viral Marketing** and **Web Marketing Basics**, when you subcribe to the FREE e-mail version of Doctor Ebiz. We respect your privacy and never sell or rent our lists. Please don't subscribe your friends. Let them decide for themselves.
>
> E-mail [   ]   Subscribe Now!
>
> Click here to **change your e-mail address** or **unsubscribe entirely**.

The first example is hoping that the site visitors will provide their own incentive and momentum. The second example shows how to go about it when you're really serious about building your list of subscribers. It gives reasons and incentives, and addresses legitimate concerns, like privacy.

Look at a dozen ecommerce sites, identify their key customer action points, and see how hard the copy works to close those actions. In the vast majority of cases, the copy doesn't work nearly hard enough. When you have low conversion rates at these action points, it impacts the total performance of your site and your business. So it's well worth taking the time to review and improve these key copy points on your own site.

Step 4

Test, test, and test again.

Testing in the offline world is a well-established practice, particularly in the area of direct marketing where its practitioners have been testing design, copy, and offers in numerous ways for decades. The driving force behind the testing done by direct marketers is the knowledge that small changes in text or even the color of a background can make a significant change in the results achieved. So far, that same healthy obsession with testing does not appear to have taken hold online. Online teams will write emails and put up text on sales pages on their sites and run them as they are without testing the copy at all. The irony here is that because of its immediacy and responsiveness, the Web is a tester's dream come true. While testing of various copy, design, and offer elements in a direct mail piece involves a time line of months, those same kinds of tests can be executed and analyzed online within a matter of days or even hours. You can test the words themselves, and you can also test the various offers they describe.

Going back to the example of the newsletter sign-up area on the Doctor Ebiz site, Dr. Wilson tried a number of different offers before arriving at the text he uses today:

> First I tried using a Palm Pilot as a prize for an incentive, but in hindsight, that wasn't targeted clearly enough at my audience. Then I tried offering free banner advertising on my site as an incentive. That worked better, but involved a lot of work at my end. Next, I tried the offer of one free ebook and that

worked better still. However, when I added another free ebook the results were even stronger, so that's what I have on my site now. I'll probably start testing that again soon to see if I can beat it.

As soon as you can secure a commitment to test key copy elements, the next task is to determine which elements to test. Here are just some of the points at which testing copy on a continuous basis can yield the best results.

- Email "Subject" lines.

- Product or service descriptions.

- Sign-up and registration forms of any kind.

- Every screen in your shopping cart.

- Link titles in emails and newsletters.

- All headings and subheads, wherever they are.

- Sig files at the end of emails and newsletters.

- All calls to action, wherever they are.

And you should be doing more than just testing the words themselves. You should test their position on the page, the color of the font, and the color of the background over which they appear. Sometimes the most innocuous change can make a significant and unexpected difference.

When you test copy, there are two fundamental rules that should be followed. First, test only one change at a time. If there is more than one variable, you'll never know which element resulted in the change in customer response. Second, be sure that you and everyone else is absolutely clear on *what* you are testing. Are you testing for a change in clickthrough from one page to another? Are you testing for an increase in sales? Are you testing for how long a user stays on a particular site page? Are you testing the pathway a user takes through your site? If you want to test more than one outcome at a time, that's fine. Test just the one variable and then measure its impact on a number of different outcomes. How many customer actions on that variable are required to give you a statistically significant result? This will vary according to your individual industry and circumstances, but a simple rule of thumb is to ensure that you have a minimum of 200 customer actions for each test. So if you are testing a link title on a newsletter and you typically get a 2 percent clickthrough on it, you will need to send out a minimum of 10,000 newsletters with that version of the title in order to receive approximately 200 responses.

While it's easiest to test small blocks of text in particular spots, don't forget to also test larger elements on your site. Right now, you might have a 15-word sentence of introductory text on your homepage that tells visitors who you are and what you do. Test that against 5 words and against 50 words. If the 50-word version wins, test that against 75 words, and so on. And if your newsletter runs at about 150 words, test it at both half and double that length. Do the same with your emails. And never stop. There's always something you can do to inch those conversion rates up a few points more.

In the world of copy, particularly in those places where a customer action is required, testing should become an absolute priority with your company. With an environment as responsive as the Web, it makes no sense not to test copy on a daily basis.

Step 5

Add personality and a unique voice wherever you can.

The Internet is a place in which you can conduct business, but it is not a marketing or advertising medium in any traditional sense. So while you build your business around high-impact copy that is written to get results, don't lose sight of the key differences that make the Web unique. The voices of individuals online are still louder than those of commerce. The dominant activity online is not buying at ecommerce sites; it's emailing and instant-messaging your friends, family, and colleagues. The Internet has expanded both the number of individuals with whom you communicate and the frequency and speed with which you do so. The Internet is more about relationships than it is about commerce. It is more a space for people to self-publish their thoughts and passions than it is a virtual mall for convenient shopping. Your site, emails, and newsletters will connect with your customers in a more powerful way if you tap into the personal, conversational nature of the Web. The first and simplest way to shift over into this new space is to make sure that your business online shows a little personality.

You can add personality through design and through voice. The voice you use online should be more personal in nature than the voice you use for offline promotions. That more personal style better fits the natural ecology of the Web. To explore, develop, and test a voice that fits both your company and your audience, it may make sense to confine your early testing within your newsletter or emails before you roll it out across all channels. Expressing your new voice first though email offers a couple of key advantages. First, their email inbox is the place in which your customers expect to find real voices and unique personalities. Second, this is also the most responsive channel through which you'll be reaching your customers, so if your voice is off-key or not credible, you can be sure that some of your readers will quickly let you know.

When determining the right voice for your company online, take your marketing hat off for a while. The voices of individuals online are recognized and respected only when they are genuine and sincere. The same is true of the voices of companies online. This isn't a sales gimmick. This is about digging deep through the layers of corporate-speak and finding a human voice that really can represent your company. Few companies get it right. You need a voice that speaks to your own corporate culture, but also resonates with your customers.

When you get it right, when you find a voice that works for both yourself and your customers and prospects, you can and should then start to apply that voice across all your online channels. You need to speak with one voice, wherever that voice is heard. It makes little sense to have your site sound one way and your customer service agents sound quite different. Even your product descriptions should carry traces of your voice, so they can be recognized as being an expression of the same personality that shines through in your emails. Building this voice and personality across multiple channels is a large task and entails the training of more than just company writers.

If the development and integration of a unique, personal voice across your online business sounds like a daunting task, take comfort in the fact that the end benefit will justify the struggle. Not only will a personal voice help your company connect more easily with your customers online and hold their attention and loyalty for longer, but it will also represent your best defense against the competition. Competitors may be able to duplicate your products, services, pricing, and offers, but they won't be able to duplicate your voice.

If this sounds like a long-term win rather than an easy win, you can get started very simply by slowly developing and testing some variations in your voice through your email and newsletter programs. It's easy to get started.

Step 6

Use newsletters to build relationships.

This point leads on from the last. Newsletters are not only the best medium through which to try out and evolve your online voice; they are also number one when it comes to creating relationships. A strong newsletter can be an editorial haven within a storm of sales and promotion. This is the neutral ground over which you can communicate with your customers in a manner that is nonadversarial and speaks only to your desire and ability to add value to their lives in some small way. Right now, most of the best newsletters are put out by content-related sites or individual enthusiasts who use them as an avenue to self-publish their views and passions. It's rare to find a great newsletter being published by an online retailer. One exception is the newsletter put out by mySEASONS.com, a major gardening site. The company sells plants, seeds, gardening accessories, and gifts, and it also publishes information-packed newsletters. Here's the opening to just one of them:

mySEASONS Regional Gardening News

With the planting season in full swing, it's hard to know where to start in the garden. Our team of 14 regional gardening experts will help you make the right choices in your garden bloom with gardening tips, designs, and expert advice for your region.

The company offers 14 different versions of the newsletter, depending on where in the United States you live. There's no promotional content, just solid advice on how to grow a great garden. That's a lot of work for newsletters that don't appear to generate any direct revenue. So where's the value for mySEASONS? The company is building strong relationships with its subscribers. The greater the value of the information it provides, the deeper the loyalty it creates and the more likely those subscribers are to make their garden purchases from the mySEASONS site.

Whatever your business, you'll have information that your customers will find of value. You sell mineral water? So produce a newsletter on healthy diets. You sell printing services to small companies? So produce a newsletter on marketing ideas for small business. The newsletter doesn't have to be exactly on the subject of your product or service. It simply has to have appropriate content that delivers real value to its readers. Over time, your readers will come to respect you as a source of honest information and will be more likely to choose you when it comes to making a purchase.

Step 7

Keep serving your customers after the sale.

This may be as simple as changing the text on the confirmation email that is sent out after a transaction is completed on your site. Most such messages are cold and factual and ignore the state of mind of the purchaser. Particularly for those who have purchased from you for the first time, that email arrives at a moment of considerable nervousness. "Did my order actually get through? Is my credit card information safe? Will I actually receive what I purchased?"

This is a good place at which to insert a human, personal voice that is reassuring to the reader. Let your customers know that they're not dealing with a faceless corporation. Help them feel that real people are watching out for them and are always available to help them when necessary. Say thank you. Sign the email with the name of a person. Let customers know what to expect and when to expect it. Remind them of your guarantees and returns policy. Make them feel good about their purchase!

Another spot where many online retailers miss a key opportunity, time and again, is in the cardboard box that carries the product itself. Insert a note that tells your customer how much you appreciate his business. Have someone sign it by hand.

The first purchase that someone makes from your site will very rarely be profitable for you. It's when the person comes back several times that you stand a chance of getting back those customer acquisition costs and turning a profit. So you need to treat that first sale not as a result, but as a first step. Keep the sales path open, make the customers feel good about your site, and prime them for the next purchase.

Step 8

Tell people what your site is about.

You know what your site is all about, and so does everyone else in your company. Your customers and regular visitors also know what to expect. But what about people who come to your site for the first time? Is there anywhere on the homepage that spells out exactly what your site is for and what it does? Remember, on the Web it's a great deal easier to leave your site than it is to find it again. Of all those people who came to your site, stayed a few seconds, and then left, a hefty proportion will have given up on you simply because they couldn't quickly figure out what it is you do. And why should they? Why should the burden be on your visitors? It's your responsibility to make the purpose and value of your site crystal clear to your first-time visitors. Here are a few examples of how sites get it right:

iPrint.com

Professional Printing Over The Internet. Save
Time and Money. Guaranteed!

The description of what iPrint.com does and what it promises is dead center on the page, where visitors are most likely to look first. It's a simple line that tells people exactly what they can expect:

HandheldCanada.com

Welcome to HandheldCanada.com, your Canadian source for Pocket PC's, handheld computers, pda's, modems and wireless communications from top manufacturers. Whether you prefer Windows CE or Palm you can find it at HandheldCanada.com. Browse our categories at left or jump straight to any item of interest below. Enjoy your visit!

No question here. You know exactly what the company offers and where you can expect to find it:

Gorp.com

Your Guide to Outdoor Recreation & Active Travel.

Pretty brief, but still very useful. Far too often, site owners just assume that the purpose and content of their site will be obvious. In the case of Gorp.com it would have been easy to assume that the various headings and photos on the homepage would be enough to alert new users to the fact that the site is about travel. True, but why expect the users to see and read a patchwork of different clues in order to figure out what you could have told them anyway? In addition, the copy line above takes things a little further and positions the site as being focused on a particular type of travel.

Finally, here are the introductory lines on the Geezer.com Web site. Sometimes, a simple and plain description is all you need:

Welcome to Geezer.com—a virtual marketplace offering thousands of handcrafted products from America's senior artisans.

Almost every site would benefit from a few descriptive words on the homepage. They're an easy thing to add and will certainly reduce the attrition rate you currently experience with your homepage visitors.

Step 9

Make the sale.

Take a look at the copy used to describe your products and services at the point of purchase. Is the copy strong enough? Does it drive the prospect forward? Does it say enough? On many sites, the answer to all three of these questions is no. One of the simplest tasks you can start on now is to make sure that the text says enough to answer all the questions swirling around in your customers' heads. It's tempting to keep it brief, but if you don't say enough, your visitors won't have enough information to feel secure about making the purchase. And if the text doesn't have a little zip and enthusiasm, your visitors may not feel that they *want* to make the purchase.

Here's an example of text from a camera site that gets the balance just right:

- **Sleek & Compact** Canon Know-How has developed a way to make the steely S300 leaner and meaner than its rivals. At 3.7 x 2.5 x 1.2 inches and a scant 8.5 oz., this latest Digital ELPH is the world's smallest and lightest 3X zoom digital camera. The high-tech textured steel casing is as rugged as it is attractive. The beauty of PowerShot lies not only in what you see but also in what you don't.

- **High Image Quality** Canon technology gives the S300 a 1/2.7 inch type, 2.11 megapixel CCD, able to record a 1600x1200 pixel image.

This is just part of the sales copy. The style of text works well, giving both the technical information your prospects need and that feel-good sensation that comes with knowing that this would be a very cool purchase. It appeals to the prospect's head and to his heart.

Attention should also be paid to those screens within the shopping cart itself. A significant percentage of sales are lost within those pages. There are usability issues that contribute to those losses, but it is also about the copy. Once a customer is delivered into the shopping cart area on a site, it's as if the copywriter feels her job is done. Not so. The cold, bleak landscape of those interminable screens and forms could very definitely benefit from some brief, but reassuring, text. You could even show some testimonials from happy customers over on the right side. Something like that wouldn't interfere with the flow of the checkout process, but would add elements of warmth and reassurance to an otherwise chilly environment.

Step 10

Refresh all the old text that lingers in dark corners.

Web sites and email programs evolve unevenly. You probably update your homepage a great deal more frequently than your privacy policy page. Your promotional emails will be changed and refreshed more often than those emails that are generated automatically by customer actions at your site. In other words, where you attempt to reach your customers most frequently is where you update your copy the most. But what about those automated emails? When did you last check that text? When did you last check the tone of the copy on the page that describes your shipping policies?

The uneven evolution of copy across your online presence can create all kinds of problems for you. First, inaccuracies can creep in. You might update your privacy policy and immediately make changes to the text on the privacy policy page. But what about that reference to privacy in your

FAQ area? And what about that drag-and-drop text that your customer service people use?

Inaccuracies of fact are, one hopes, not too hard to catch. But inconsistencies of voice and tone are harder to track and harder to deal with, unless you're paying very close attention.

Think about those pages on your site that haven't been updated for the last six months. Get printouts of all the emails that are sent automatically and all the customer service text that is dragged and dropped. When you read these through, you may well find that some inaccuracies have crept in over the months. But you'll also find that the tone of much of this text has lagged behind the tone of the copy on your homepage and in your promotional emails. The copy you write will naturally evolve over time, even when you don't deliberately plan for it to happen. When this occurs, a distance appears between the text in frequently updated parts of your site and the text in more static areas.

Why is it a problem when the tone of your copy evolves unevenly? Because it brings a discord to your voice. You begin to speak in a number of different "tongues." When your customers sense that, when they feel that there is more than one voice at play, they may start to feel uncomfortable. And when your customers begin to feel uncomfortable, their sense of trust becomes diluted.

To avoid uneven evolution of your copy, simply mark your calendar two or three times a year for a complete copy "spring-cleaning." Not only will you catch mistakes of fact and inconsistencies in tone, but you will also have a chance to find places where the copy just isn't working hard enough.

Copy is never done—it's never finished. Keep track of what you write and go back to all of it, time and again, to make sure that it's as good as it can be.

CHAPTER SIXTEEN

AN ONLINE WRITER'S MANIFESTO

The craft of copywriting online is in its infancy. It is a creative skill that is not practiced enough and is barely recognized at all. That's great news for those who want to make their mark as one of the new generation of great copywriters online. Now is the time.

Honesty Is at the Core of All Great Copywriting.

Scamming your audience is easy. A few buzzwords, a contest, and a photograph of a tropical paradise will do it every time. But that's not how you build a loyal customer base. Trust and loyalty spring only from absolute honesty. Besides, being honest makes it a lot easier to write great copy. Confine yourself to the truth and you won't be distracted by numerous shades of gray. Honesty keeps you on track, in pursuit of a single truth that serves both your customers and your company.

Cynics Will Never Make Great Online Copywriters.

If you take pleasure in the manipulation of an audience and you laugh at people's gullibility and foolishness, you don't have the makings of a great copywriter online. You might have the writing skills. You might know how to crank up response rates. You might make a pile of money. But you'll never know the pleasure of crafting a message that truly adds value to both your customers and your company. You'll never show your spouse and family what you wrote and be able to say with pride, "I wrote that."

Copywriting Is a Creative Process.

Copywriting is as creative as designing, painting, programming, or the writing of fiction. The writing of great copy is a creative process. As with any act of creation, you work within limitations. Paint a picture and you're limited by the size of your canvas. Write a sonnet and you're restricted by the demands of the rhyming iambic pentameter. Write great copy and you have to serve the needs of both your company and your audience. Finding that point of intersection takes time, insight, and creativity.

Great Copywriters Are Great Marketers.

Copywriters do more than translate the creative brief into the words on a screen or a sheet of paper. Great copywriters are also great marketers, intuitively if not by formal training. They have to be. Without the insight of a marketer, how can a copywriter write copy that truly addresses the marketing needs of the company?

It's the Words That Make the Sale.

Flash animations don't make sales. CRM software doesn't make sales. Pictures of products don't make sales. If you have trouble believing that, remove all the words from your site and see how many sales you make. Without great copy, your online presence is dead in the water. It's the words that open, build, and close the sale.

It's the Words That Build Relationships.

Not even the highest-priced personalization software can be personal without great copy. It's the words, not the technology, that connect with customers. So why is so much investment made in the software and so little made in the message itself? Without words, there can be no relationships, no personal messages, no personality.

Copywriters Cannot Succeed without the Support and Respect of Their Colleagues.

Traditionally, in the world of offline advertising, a copywriter would be paired with an art director or designer. Successful teams carried all the hallmarks of a sometimes dysfunctional, but oddly successful, marriage. The team was better than the sum of its parts. Copywriters would sometimes make great design suggestions. Designers would sometimes write great headlines. They would fight; they would make up. This team would also work closely with typographers, photographers, illustrators, and printers. The creation of great work was absolutely dependent on mutual respect among all the parties involved. This was how great advertising was created.

For copywriters to create great copy online, they need to be part of a similar team, based on equal respect for all parties. Without that respect, the team is nothing. Without the team, your online efforts remain a jigsaw of individual contributions, no part quite fitting with any other. Without a strong team, the whole will be less than the sum of the individual parts.

Copywriters Are the Natural Architects of Your Online Presence.

The Web is a text-based environment. That's how the Net started out, just with words. That's how the Web is today, with billions of messages passing between millions of individuals online, every day of the year. For users of the Web, text is the simplest and fastest way to receive and understand your message.

If text is the message carrier of choice online—the choice of the users, not necessarily the experts—copywriters must be encouraged to play a key role in the development of your online presence. When it's all about words, you need great wordsmiths.

Great Copywriting Takes Time.

It's a given that programmers need time to do their work. It's accepted that designers need time to be creative and time to find both their inspiration and its best creative execution. So why are copywriters expected to write great copy as quickly as a manager can write a Monday-morning memo?

Great copy takes time. It takes time for the writer to find the right thing to say. And it takes time to write and rewrite, again and again, until the right thing is said in the right way.

Online Copy Cannot Be Cut and Pasted from Your Offline Channels.

To hand a development team the copy from a brochure or offline sales letter and say, "Hey, use this," shows an absolute misunderstanding of how text works online and a total disrespect for the writer. The copy for a site, for a newsletter, for emails, and for live chat all needs to be custom-written with the unique environment of the Web in mind. Copywriters who are asked to shoehorn offline copy into the Web should hold tight to their pride and politely refuse.

Support Young Copywriters Online.

In 20 years' time, when you look back at the great online copywriters, you will see a mixture of writers who came to the Web from a career offline and those who started their copywriting careers online. This latter group, the younger writers, are the ones who are trying to get a toehold online right now. When a young writer expresses an interest in copywriting online, he or she should be encouraged and provided with the best support and training available. These young writers will have a profound impact on the success of business online. They will have grown up with the Web. The Web's culture will be in their veins, and they will understand it in ways that older writers will find hard to match.

Pay Copywriters What They Are Worth.

Salary levels are signposts for young people coming to the Web. At high school and at college they will look to see where the money is. If it's in programming, that's where many will go. If it's in design, more great designers will come online. And if you want great copywriters online, you need to give that skill the recognition it deserves. Good online copywriters deserve a good salary. While money is rarely the sole motivation for someone choosing a particular career, it certainly makes an impact. Talented people want recognition. They want a decent title. They want a good office. They want all the signposts that say, "This is an important and highly valued job."

Even the Best Copywriters Need a Good Briefing.

The last member of the creative team in an offline ad agency is the account executive or manager. This is the person who crafts the creative brief. While not viewed as being part of the creative department, the account person has a huge impact on how good a job the creative group can do.

Can an architect build a great building if he doesn't know what it's for? Can a designer design a site interface if she doesn't know who will be coming to the site and what they hope to achieve there? Can a copywriter write good copy without a full briefing on the purpose of the text and the audience to which it is directed?

When the brief is poor, it's hard, if not impossible, to produce great creative work, offline or online. Don't expect great work from your copywriters if they don't get a great briefing at the outset of the project.

Study the Work of Great Copywriters.

You may have a natural talent for copywriting, but you'll never become a great copywriter until you have studied the work of those who came before you. You can never stop learning. When you think you know it all, you stagnate.

Study the work of the offline greats, like David Ogilvy, Rosser Reeves, Bill Bernbach, Leo Burnett, Ed McCabe, David Abbot, Bob Levenson, Andrew Ruherford, Tony Brignull, Jim Durfee, Neil French, and Barbara Nokes. And then look out for the new online greats, as and where you find them.

Become One of the First Great Online Copywriters.

The great offline copywriters of the past can teach today's writers how to master their craft and take pride in what they do. But none of those people can teach you the unique demands of copywriting online. Much is the same between offline and online copywriting. But even if the differences make up just 10 percent of the whole, it's those differences that make online copywriting unique. It's not business as usual on the Net, nor is it copywriting as normal. Take what you can from the offline world and weave it into the new. Stand up and carve out your place as a copywriter in the online world.

INDEX

Index

Index

Index